SURF BREAKING AGAINST THE OUTER BARRIER

RINGS OF PACIFIC SURF AROUND ONE TREE ISLAND

JAGGED CORALS ON PICKERSGILL REEF AT LOW TIDE

SEAGULLS FLYING AGAINST A FIERY SUNSET

MANTA RAY IN UNDULATING UNDERWATER "FLIGHT"

PROJECTING "TONGUES" OF BRAMPTON ISLAND

OTHER TIME-LIFE SERIES

LIFE NATURE LIBRARY
LIFE SCIENCE LIBRARY
GREAT AGES OF MAN
FOODS OF THE WORLD
TIME-LIFE LIBRARY OF ART
LIFE LIBRARY OF PHOTOGRAPHY
THE EMERGENCE OF MAN
THE OLD WEST
THE ART OF SEWING

THE GREAT BARRIER REEF

THE WORLD'S WILD PLACES/TIME-LIFE BOOKS/AMSTERDAM

BY CRAIG McGREGOR
AND THE EDITORS OF TIME-LIFE BOOKS

TIME-LIFE BOOKS

Editorial Staff for *The Great Barrier Reef*:
EDITOR: John Man
Deputy Editor: Simon Rigge
Picture Editors: Jean Tennant, Pamela Marke
Design Consultant: Louis Klein
Staff Writers:
Heather Wyatt, Tony Long
Picture Researcher: Kerry Arnold
Art Director: Graham Davis
Design Assistant: Joyce Mason
Editorial Assistant: Vanessa Kramer

Consultants
Zoology: Dr. P. J. K. Burton
Invertebrates: Dr. Michael Tweedie
Botany: Phyllis Edwards
Geology: Dr. Peter Stubbs
Ichthyology: Dr. Alwyne Wheeler
Ornithology: I. J. Ferguson-Lees

Published by Time-Life International (Nederland) B.V.
5 Ottho Heldringstraat, Amsterdam 18

Craig McGregor was brought up in the Australian bush and began studying its wild life from an early age. Since then he has written many books on Australia, including *The High Country*, *Profile of Australia* and *Life in Australia*. He was awarded a Commonwealth Literary Fund Fellowship, the Xavier Society Prize for Literature and, in 1969, a Harkness Fellowship, which enabled him to study, travel and write articles and film scripts in the United States.

Brian Rosen, the consultant on this book, is one of few scientists to specialize in coral biology. He studied geology at the Universities of Oxford and London and wrote his doctoral thesis on Seychelles corals. Dr. Rosen taught at the University of Wales, Aberystwyth, and was Research Associate at the School of Physics, Newcastle-upon-Tyne. He is now in charge of fossil corals at the British Museum of Natural History, London.

The Cover: Above the shadowed, grey-specked sand of a coral island on the Great Barrier Reef, a light noon breeze stirs the fronds of a dead pandanus palm. A ripple of surf marks the point where the sea washes over the island's protective girdle of coral reef.

Contents

A Sunken Rampart

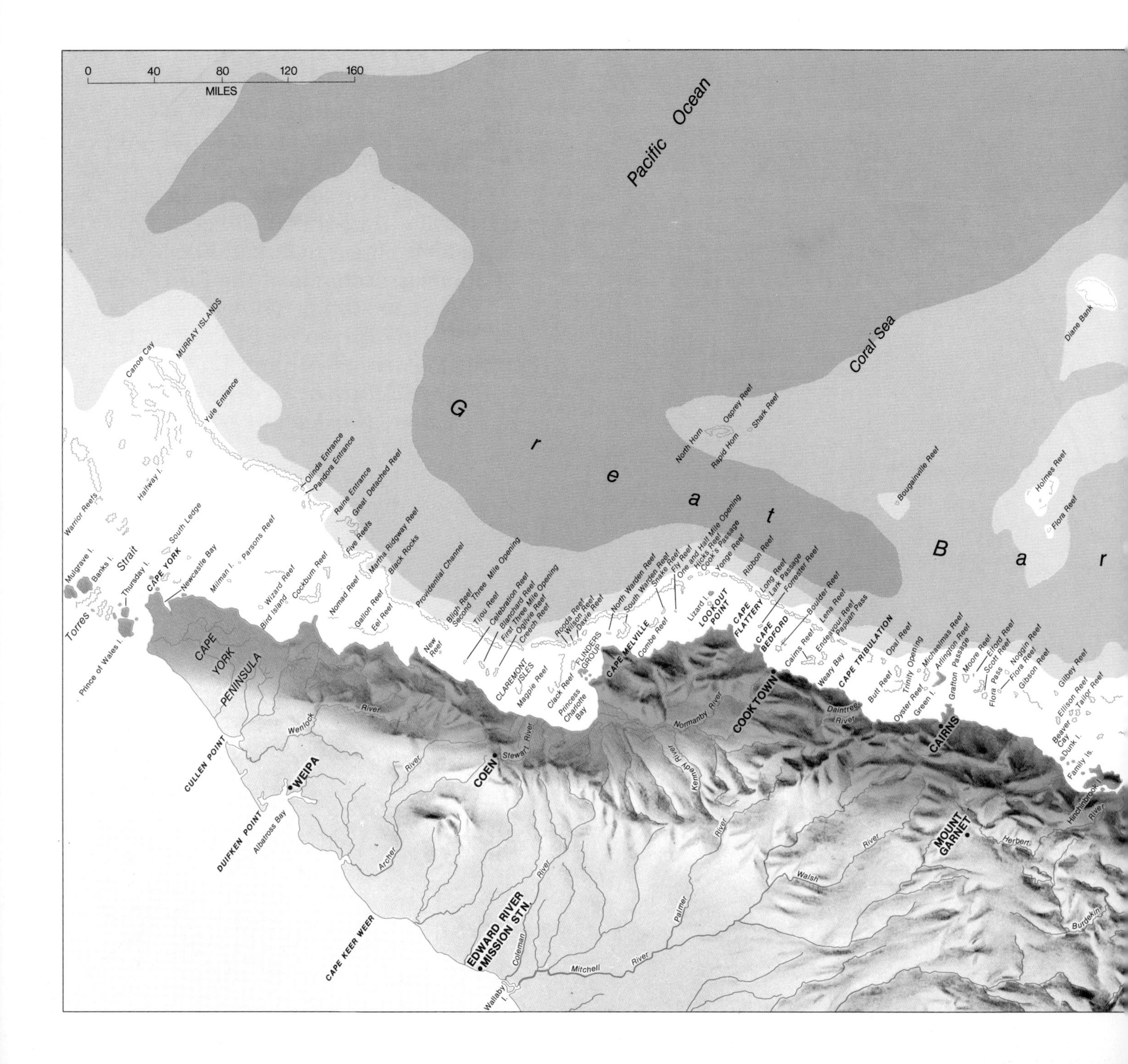

The region of the Great Barrier Reef, a sea-girt wilderness (blue rectangle right) of coral reefs, cays, islands and sheltered seas, forms a 100,000-square-mile fringe to the eastern Australian mainland. This huge maritime province, resting on a continental shelf no more than 600 feet deep (shown white in the detailed map below), ends wherever darker blues indicate the progressively deeper waters of the Coral Sea and the Pacific Ocean. It stretches 1,260 miles from the Murray Islands in the Torres Strait south to the Capricorn group of coral cays. On its eastern border is the mighty Barrier itself, an almost continuous wall of coral limestone that, below Cooktown, breaks down into more widely scattered reefs. West of the Barrier is a lagoon channel specked with islands (green), the sunken peaks of the mountain chain that lines the coast.

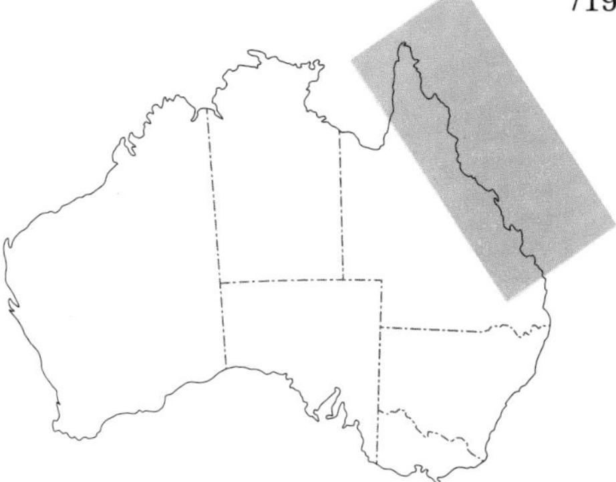

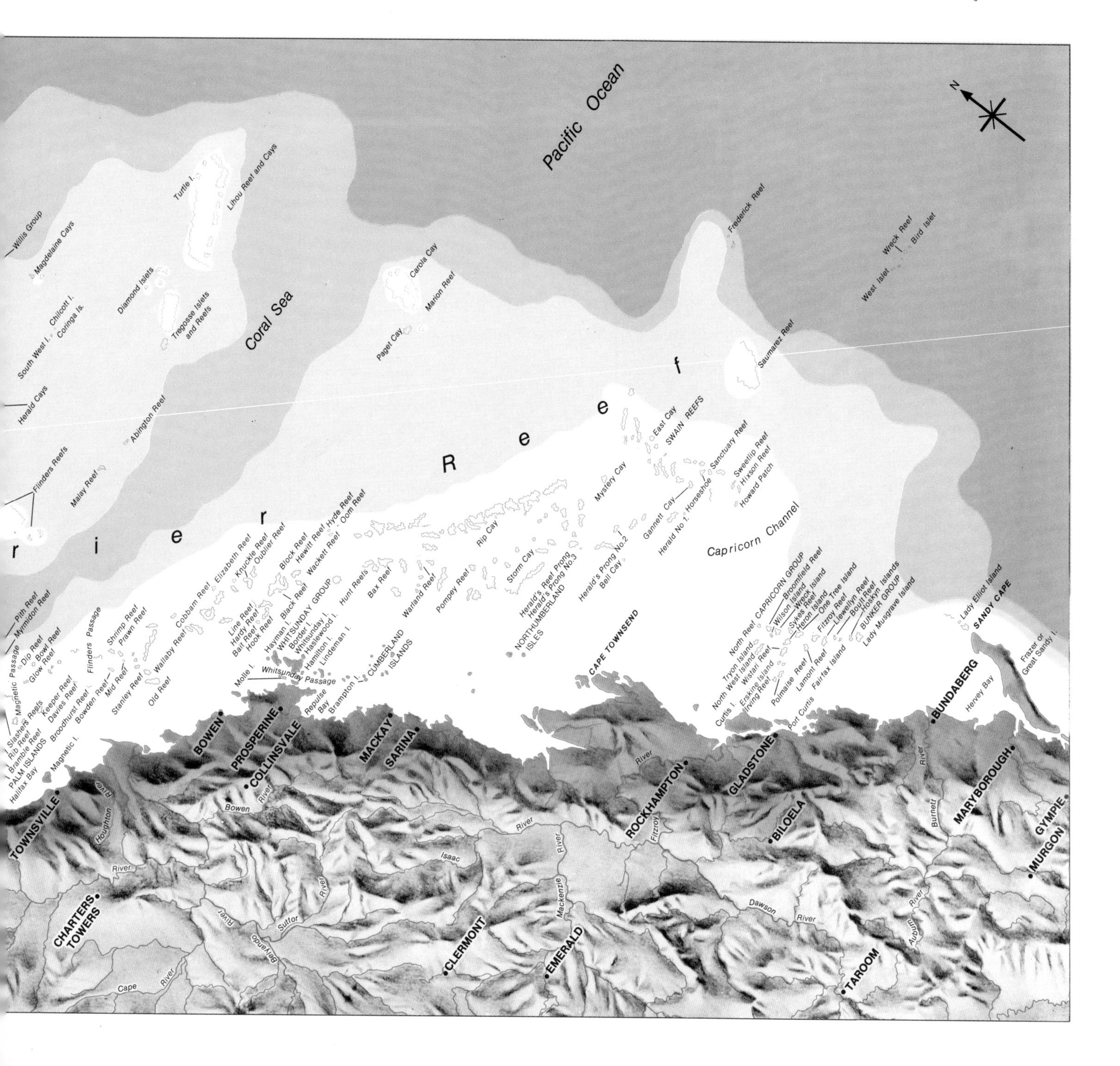

1/ Fringe of a Continent

A reef such as one speaks of here is scarcely known in Europe. It is a wall of coral rock rising perpendicular out of the unfathomable ocean. CAPTAIN JAMES COOK/ *JOURNAL OF THE "ENDEAVOUR"*

The helicopter leaves the Australian mainland at Gladstone, an industrial, sub-tropical port stained red with bauxite. The harbour, a blue inlet splattered with pancake-like islands and backed by low mountains, falls behind. Ahead, north-east of the Queensland coast, lies the dull, metallic blue of the Pacific Ocean: from this height the waves look like shallow wrinkles on the surface of the sea, giving a misleading air of calm, and the horizon is a long, unbroken arc. The cockpit is filled with noise from the rotors, a high-pitched shrieking like cicadas in high summer. Droplets of moisture slide along the outside of the windows. It is hot, and I can feel the perspiration trickling down my chest. Both the pilot and I are wearing thick, canvas life jackets. We are heading 45 miles out over the sea to a point in the world's largest coral wilderness, the Great Barrier Reef.

Twenty minutes later, a slice of white appears on the horizon. It looks like a beach in mid-ocean. As we draw closer, iridescent green streaks appear in the sea, trailing for a few miles away to the right; they are patches of coral lying just beneath the surface of the water. Then the slice of white swells, takes shape and becomes a deserted coral island, shaped in the form of a boomerang. The white is indeed a beach, encircling a small forest of palms and tropical trees gathered at the island's centre.

In the distance ahead of us, I can see more land breaking the surface. This is our destination: a larger and more spectacular island, Heron, one of the 13 islands in the Capricorn group. It looks almost exactly as imagination dictates a lonely Pacific coral island should look: dark green, ringed by an oval of sheer white sand and set within a series of looping underwater reefs. The helicopter sinks lower towards the island, hovers and settles down on the beach. I stumble from the cockpit, partly blinded by the sun reflecting off the sand. The shimmering glare has a brilliance that stabs at the eyes and reduces my first impressions to a series of flashes: the stilted roots of pandanus palms clinging to the ocean's edge; thousands of noddy terns cawing in the grey-trunked pisonia trees; and the over-powering, sun-rotten stench peculiar to tropical islands, a combination of decaying vegetation, over-ripe fruit and bird droppings.

I had arrived on the Great Barrier Reef—or at least, one of its far southern constituents. The white slice of island, the green streaks in the water, Heron Island itself and its sisters are all parts of "the Reef". For although its name suggests a long massive rampart—an impression reinforced by the long wavy blue line picked out on many small-scale maps—it is far more complex than that: a maze of innumerable coral reefs, cays and lagoons, rocky inshore islands and deep channels, underwater caverns and shallow pools that together form a huge maritime province covering 100,000 square miles. It stretches in a long strip for 1,260 miles along Australia's eastern coast, extending from the Torres Strait at the northern tip of the continent to just south of the Tropic of Capricorn, which actually bisects Heron Island. From the coastline it extends out to sea for up to 200 miles, while the underlying continental shelf restricts the depth of water to generally less than 30 fathoms before dropping like a precipice into the deep Pacific. At the eastern edge, separated from the mainland by the deep lagoon channel over which I had flown, stand the great chains of outermost reefs that give the Barrier its name.

The innumerable separate reefs—of which there are thought to be about 2,500 identifiable ones—take up about a third of the entire region. They can be small patch reefs no larger than a table-top or great reef formations up to 20 square miles in area. They can be fathoms deep or so close to the surface that waves froth over them. Along the line of the outermost reefs, the ocean swells rolling in from the Pacific break in an almost continuous line of surf.

From a vast series of reefs in the Torres Strait, the main Reef stretches southward, narrowing until at Cape Melville—where the continental shelf also narrows—both the intervening channel and the reefs themselves are no more than ten miles across. Further south again, past Cooktown in the central region of the Reef, the channel widens greatly, containing many reefs as well as rocky islands. These central and northern regions, where the Reef drops steeply away into oceanic depths, mark the true "barrier". In the southern section, south of Mackay, the shelf widens still further and the "barrier" breaks down into many widely scattered coral formations ending with the Swain Reefs some 100 miles out to sea.

Rising above the reefs are the coral cays or keys. Like Heron Island, they began as reefs, perhaps partially exposed at low tide, but covered by the waves twice a day. Over the years, sand and coral debris were washed and blown on to them, slowly accumulating, until the reefs emerged permanently from the sea. Then they were colonized with plants from seeds carried by wind, birds and sea.

To describe these cays as above-water is not saying very much. Approaching one of them by sea is a strange experience, quite unlike approaching other islands or the mainland. I was once in a fishing boat, sailing to North-West Island, another member of the Capricorn group, and we were steering east-south-east. I had tried to sleep on deck that night, because the small cabin was crowded and stuffy and reeked of the shark skins that had been stowed in the forward hold on a previous trip. Now, just before dawn, I was wedged up front between the cabin and the guard rail, soaked by some squall-driven rain an hour or so before and leaden with early morning fatigue. When dawn came I peered sleepily at the horizon, looking for our island which should have been appearing by now. But there was nothing to be seen. Perhaps we had been blown off course by the squalls.

By breakfast time, the light and visibility had improved but there was still no island. Breakfast was rather meagre and makeshift; I wondered whether we had enough provisions to make a longer voyage than expected. For the first time I had a real sense of what it must have been like in the 18th Century for early explorers such as Captain Cook, sailing up the east coast of Australia where no European had sailed before, waiting for the next landfall, not knowing whether it would be tomorrow or next week, peaceful or fiercely inhospitable.

At last, the lookout shouted that the island was in sight. Within a short time I too could see a distant smudge lying slightly to starboard. As we drew closer I could make out a dark group of blue-grey blotchy shapes which, astonishingly, gradually parted company with the line of

Changing colours in an aerial photograph chart the elements making up a typical reef, Wistari, in the Capricorn group. On the right is the indigo blue of the deep Pacific, bordered by a light blue band marking shallower water that covers the reef slope. A white line of surf edges the dark grey rim of the reef. The adjoining band of light grey is living coral, while to its left are streaks of dead coral leading to a broad stretch of submerged sand. The light blue lagoon waters farther left cover smaller coral reefs. In the distance, other coral breaks the surface.

the horizon and rose to hover like an apologetic mirage above the limit of the water. If the crew had not so completely accepted this trick, I would have been convinced that I was witnessing some weird meteorological phenomenon rather than glimpsing a solid coral cay.

The captain brought out a rubbed and tattered chart, looking at least as old as one of Cook's, and pored over it with some of his crew. After some discussion he came and said that it was, indeed, our island. The blue-grey smudges, he explained, were the tops of palm trees.

For something like an hour we watched as they began to fall into focus. They became greener and it was easier to see now that they might be treetops, though they still had a strangely disembodied appearance. As we drew closer, the greenery gradually turned into recognizable foliage attached to the horizon by fine vertical lines—tree trunks. The island itself now emerged from the line of the horizon, a floating disc of sand and forest. I could see a white line below the trees—surf pounding on the reef edge, a surging mass that spoke of the rugged teeth of the reef below. From what depth of memory he drew, I cannot imagine, but with no apparent indication that it would be safe, the captain brought the boat hard round and we glided into a calm anchorage.

Coral islands that are known as well as this are something of an exception, since most of the cays of the Great Barrier Reef—let alone the underwater coral jungle—are virtually untouched, their exact number as yet unknown. Official maps still bear spaces labelled "Unexamined but Considered Dangerous to Navigation". In spite of the many apparent openings in the line of outer reefs, ships generally pass through it only at two recognized channels—Trinity Opening opposite Cairns and Flinders Passage near Townsville. Even in small boats, only a few skilled skippers and fishermen attempt to navigate complex mazes such as the Swain Reefs. Often they must race the sharply-dropping tides in order to clear the coral in safety.

In summer, between November and February, there is the additional hazard of the monsoons. Heavy rains beat down, obscuring sea and sky under one heavy, dark cloud bank. Occasionally the Reef is struck by cyclones, hurricane-force winds that sweep in from the Coral Sea, whipping up immense waves and leaving stained muddy seas strewn with debris. They wash away some of the smaller cays completely and also attack the underwater reefs, tearing up corals from the sea floor, shattering them against one another and piling up fragments as rubble, so producing dramatic changes in Reef geography overnight.

The Barrier has endured such depredations for centuries. Yet it is not destroyed, for it is a living, self-repairing entity. It is the largest organic structure ever built, the creation of millions upon millions of living organisms, both animals and plants. The major builders are the coral animals, known as polyps. Soft and fleshy, like sea anemones, but mostly no more than half an inch long, each one forms an external cup-like skeleton of limestone that, in most cases, becomes attached to already existing coral rock. After attachment, most coral polyps and the skeletons they form, divide to create elaborate colonies. These are stony masses or elaborate branching growths from a few inches to many feet across, that are loosely referred to as "corals". They assume a bewildering variety of shapes—branching antlers, plates, fans and hemispherical masses, some of them with convoluted surfaces resembling the human brain. Each is characteristic of a particular group of corals although some shapes are modified by the conditions under which the corals grow. Building continually upwards, the polyps gradually construct the Reef towards the water surface.

Corals dominate these shallow waters above the continental shelf because conditions are ideal. The polyps need tropical waters with temperatures higher than 20 degrees centigrade and with adequate light. They require a hard surface on which minute coral larvae, produced by them in millions, can settle. They need well oxygenated water containing adequate supplies of the small planktonic animals on which they feed. They also like clear water because, apart from reducing the light, any heavy rain of sediment would smother them. All these requirements are met in the shallow waters off the coast of Queensland over a larger area than anywhere else in the world.

But this is only a beginning: the coral framework which is constantly growing and changing underwater provides shelter for an extraordinary diversity of marine life: sponges, anemones, crawling worms and tube-dwelling worms; starfish and sea urchins; shrimps, crabs and lobsters; cowries, spider shells and cones; clams, oysters and mussels; snappers, flagtails and millions of other fish, as well as soft, leathery "corals" that, although similar to the reef-building polyps, do not create hard, limestone skeletons for themselves.

All these organisms are enmeshed in a series of complex interrelationships. The general features are straightforward enough. Most of the Reef fish are carnivores, feeding off other fish: sharks eat snappers, which eat mackerels, which eat herrings, which eat thousands of small fry each day. The whole series of relationships can be drawn in the mind's eye like a pyramid, the tiny creatures forming the base as fodder for progressively larger, but fewer, creatures further up towards the pyramid's tip. But this is just the outline. There are many other relationships and cross-relationships. Alpheid shrimps, for example, are linked with gobiid fish, not as predator and prey, but by the burrow they share for shelter. Cleaner fish are connected with other larger fish by their function of cleaning off parasites, and false cleaners by their imitation of this role for the purposes of taking predatory bites.

So bizarre and complicated are the interrelationships that, in the words of Dr. Frank H. Talbot, the director of the Australian Museum, "they would make the largest computer in the world blanch". His statement was not made lightly. It was based on the frustrating experience of 40 biologists and two computer specialists who, under the auspices of the Smithsonian Institution of Washington, tried to plan a computer simulation of feeding patterns on the Reef. They fed in the name, "address" or habitat and diet of as many individual creatures as they were aware of, hoping that the computer would be able to trace through the relationships in detail. But they failed. They were forced to conclude that years of research were necessary to bridge gaps in existing knowledge before even the crudest computer model could be drawn up.

In this, an underwater jungle, the Reef creatures have exploited every conceivable niche of habitat and lifestyle, and their adaptations for warfare are no less varied than their feeding habits. One of their most effective weapons is poison, used both for attack and defence. The box jellyfish, also known as the sea-wasp, an almost invisible bell-shaped creature, has stinging cells on its tentacles that instantly paralyse its prey—prawns and similar small animals—and can kill a man within five minutes. The cone snail is as ingenious as it is dangerous. It injects venom by way of minute arrow-like teeth stored in an internal sac and pushed one by one through a tube that pokes out of its shell like the barrel of a rifle.

Less aggressive creatures have developed extraordinary defence mechanisms. Starfish simply regrow arms that have been lopped off or damaged by predators, and brittle stars go a stage further by casting off one of their arms, perhaps as a decoy, while they retreat to cover and grow a new one. Some tubeworms even take survival to the point of suicide. If attacked they literally throw themselves to pieces, a tactic that deprives their enemies of a meal and has evolved presumably as a means of teaching predators that tubeworms are not worth feeding on.

The richness of marine life provides food for millions of birds that

Myriad colours on the underside of a coral boulder reveal a teeming population of clinging invertebrates and plants. A rare, red starfish (right) straddles encrusting grey colonial ascidians. Moving anti-clockwise, a grey linckia starfish bridges the space between red and yellow sponges. Farther left, a white-ringed money cowrie guards its mass of creamy eggs. Below these, past more red and yellow sponges, lie a small, mottled cowrie and a slug-like scutus, its black mantle encircling a white, limpet-like shell. The red specks scattered over the surface of the boulder are algae.

congregate on the remote coral cays, forming the largest seabird colonies in the world. Apart from these birds, however, most of the above-water Reef has had few residents, least of all mammals. The problems of reaching inaccessible islands decreed that the commonest mammal has been the most enterprising one—man himself.

The Australian Aborigines were undoubtedly the first people to discover the Reef some time after they reached the Australian continent from southern Asia, probably by boat, 12,000 years ago. The Chinese knew of the northern and eastern coasts of Australia, which would have included the Reef region, some 2,000 years ago. In more recent times they ranged through the Reef in search of bêches-de-mer or trepangs, the fat, sausage-like sea cucumbers that are still regarded as a delicacy in many Asian countries. When the industry was at its peak, in the 18th Century, the red trepang brought high prices from the emissaries of Chinese mandarins. As that species was fished out, the greedy trepangers boiled lesser species in copper vessels until they turned red—and unwittingly poisoned the gourmets.

To penetrate the Barrier has always been hazardous, for its coral defences are formidable. Since 1770, when the pioneering Captain James Cook first explored parts of the Reef—and also damaged his ship, the *Endeavour*, near the point he named Cape Tribulation—the Great Barrier Reef has been the graveyard of more than 500 ships. One celebrated wreck was that of the Royal Navy frigate, HMS *Pandora*, which sank with the loss of 35 lives in 1791.

She was bound for England from Tahiti, carrying 14 mutineers from Captain William Bligh's famous ship, the *Bounty*, back to be tried. The prisoners were manacled on the quarterdeck in a vermin- and maggot-ridden box-prison measuring 18 feet by 11. The captain, Edward Edwards, sought an opening in the Reef at the far north near the Murray Islands. Without warning the ship was caught up in rapid currents and heavy surf, battered against the coral wall and hurled right over. Torrents of water poured in and the vessel listed heavily. The crew attempted to stop the leaks by wrapping one of the topsails around the hull, but they failed and had to fall back on feverish pumping. During the night a cannon rolled across the plunging decks, crushing a man to death; a section of rigging crashed down and killed another. Then, near dawn, the pumps gave out. All this time the mutineers were still penned in their prison. Not until the crew were abandoning ship did the captain order them to be released. One prisoner did not get out in time and went down with the ship, along with 31 members of the crew, and three more drowned as they floundered towards a distant sand bank. But ten of the mutineers survived—only to be taken in ship's boats to the Dutch East Indies and, from there, safely back to Portsmouth for court martial.

Throughout the 19th Century, even the more detailed charts that became available could do no more than pinpoint the worst hazards of the Reef. Captain Matthew Flinders, whose meticulous charting of the Reef is still the basis for many maps in use today, made this clear when he warned other captains that if they had not the courage to "thread the needle . . . amongst the reefs", they should stay away. Yet he continually accepted the risk until his own ship went down on Wreck Reef in 1803 and he was marooned for several days on "a Small Uncertainty", an uncharted sand cay 700 miles from the nearest substantial settlement at Port Jackson, now Sydney.

Only in the last decade has man begun to make his mark on the Reef and, some say, to wreck it. Australian and overseas commercial interests are pressing claims to exploit its rich limestone, mineral and oil resources. Tourists are "fossicking" for shells and corals. Polluted wastes are flowing from the towns, ports and rivers of the mainland. And yet, for most of my time on the Reef, I was not particularly aware of these threats to the Reef's existence; its beauty and danger exerted a much more powerful influence than anything man-made. There were moments when a cool dusk breeze blew in from the sea, and the shallow water over the coral turned a milky green, and the calls of the turnstones seeped into the shore with the darkness, when the Reef seemed to slide into some idyllic state. But these were moments, fragmentary and precarious, punctuating something much more constant and disquieting. For the Great Barrier Reef has the stark, oppressive quality of any true wilderness. By night, the eerie cries of the shearwaters howling in their burrows disturbed my sleep; by day, the heat settled on everything like a pall, remorseless and omnipresent. I felt exposed and vulnerable to larger forces: the sun, the salt-laden wind and the droning waves were inescapable.

Patterns of Undersea Life

The fish that populate the Great Barrier Reef's tropical waters display an extraordinary variety of colours and shapes, and some of them seem to behave in the oddest ways. But every one of these characteristics somehow helps its owner survive.

Colours are of immense value as warning or camouflage. Dangerous fish such as the red fire-fish (opposite) positively advertise their presence and scare off intruders with extravagant combinations of greens and reds. A greater number camouflage themselves with vivid bands, spots or patches that break up their outlines and create an optical illusion confusing to predators. Others are countershaded, with dark backs that merge with the sea bed when viewed from above and silvery underparts that match the shining sea surface when seen from below.

Still other fish can change colour to match their surroundings, a process carried out by chromatophores, the colour cells in the skin. The brown spotted cod, which grows to an impressive seven feet in length and weighs up to 500 pounds, is extremely adept at using this method to conceal its huge bulk. It may alter in seconds, from dark to light, plain to banded, spotted to mottled.

Shape can also be used as camouflage. The body of the venomous stonefish, for example, is bluntly built and covered with flaps and warts, so that in the mud flats and shallow tidal waters where it lives, it looks just like a weedy piece of rock or dead coral.

Some of the oddest behaviour patterns are as valuable as colours and shapes to the fish that adopt them. A number of fish live by symbiosis, an intimate and beneficial relationship between dissimilar creatures. Some small wrasse, for example, are cleaners: like the tick-bird grooming a rhinoceros, they make their living by picking parasites off other, much larger fish, unharmed by their "customers."

The clownfish, a sprightly little scavenger, takes the process a stage further: it shelters among the deadly tentacles of the giant anemone, feeding on scraps of its food or momentarily darting out to snatch passing fry or shrimps. To the clownfish, the poisonous sting of the anemone is clearly a useful defence. What advantage the anemone gets in return is unknown, but once acquainted with a little clownfish, it steadfastly refrains from harming it.

A red fire-fish glides downwards, spreading wide the surrealistic fins it sometimes uses to "walk" on the bottom. The brilliant markings along its 15-inch length are warnings to any predators that an attack would be fatal: for it carries an arsenal of venomous spines—13 down the middle of the back, three guarding the underside of the body and one on each side.

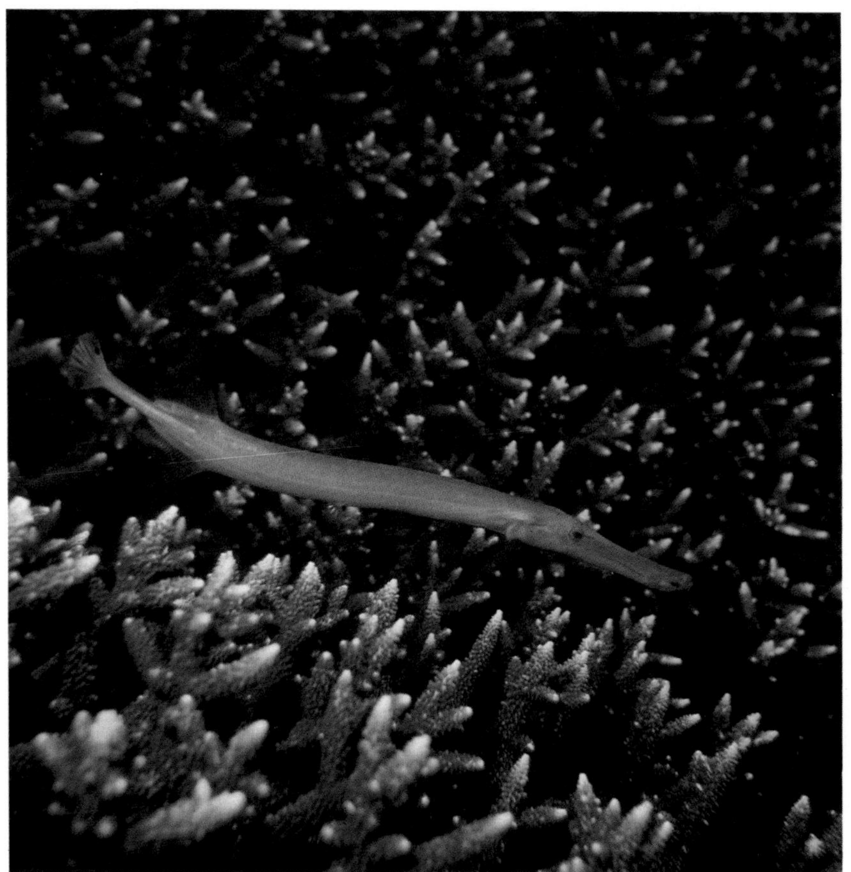

A brilliant blue angel fish (left) patrols the borders of its territory. Any other angel fish caught trespassing will be met with an aggressive exhibition of flashing colour as the owner twists and turns to reveal all its patterns. This display is usually enough warning, but a fight starts if the intruder still fails to leave.

A yard-long painted flutemouth drifts idly across a bed of staghorn coral. Propelled by almost invisible flicks of transparent fins, this trumpetfish seldom moves its body. Once in range of a small fish it need only point its head and drink in; the suction created by its extraordinary snout engulfs its prey.

A stonefish (centre) lurks among rocks and weeds, camouflaged by colour and shape.

The estuary rock cod, momentarily mottled, has a wide repertoire of pattern changes.

Close behind the gaping mouth of a moray eel, a tiny cleaner wrasse eats the parasites that infest the eel's skin, confident that it is in no danger.

Hungry snappers—notorious for their eager and voracious feeding habits—prowl the lagoon channel, constantly watching for the slightest movement that could mean food. Everything from small fishes to drifting plant fragments is fair game for the snappers. Even their shoaling behaviour is designed for superior feeding ability. Because they hunt in groups that react as a single unit, they have many pairs of eyes to scout for food and achieve far more together than they could separately.

Surprised under a favourite overhang, a coral trout turns from the intruding photographer, expressing disapproval by intensifying its colour.

A clownfish rests in safety on a stinging sea anemone.

The outline of a royal angel fish is broken by its stripes.

The harlequin tusk fish possesses large teeth capable of crushing shells.

A shoal of Moorish idols is protected by a combination of colour and behaviour. The outline of each fish is broken by the wide, dark stripes, and the shoal itself is a further confusion to predators, making it difficult to see where one fish ends and the next begins. Their name may be tied to an obscure tradition. In many parts of the Indian and Pacific Oceans, native fishermen are said to have held them in great reverence—hence their name, "Moorish" being an Anglo-Indian term for "Mohammedan". Any Moorish idols netted by these fishermen were supposedly returned to the water with an apologetic bow.

2/ Builders of the Reef

Travellers tell us of the vast dimensions of the pyramids and other great ruins, but utterly insignificant are the greatest of these, when compared to these mountains of stone.

CHARLES DARWIN/ *JOURNAL OF "ADVENTURE" AND "BEAGLE"*

It is tempting to think, as did the wide-eyed voyaging naturalists of the 17th and 18th Centuries, that the world's reefs were built by corals piling up one on top of the other until the structures were complete. One of the earliest observers to put this view was an otherwise anonymous Mr. Strachan, who devoted half a page to it in a paper he read to the Royal Society in London in 1704 and then disappeared from history. "There are great Banks of the said Coral," expounded Strachan; "it is porous neither so firm and smooth as the upright, which grows in little Branches, and when they are come to the full growth, there grows other betwixt these, and then upon these grows others, until it is become like a Rock for thickness."

Mr. Strachan's views on the subject were brief and, for the time, to the point. But one wonders if he ever attempted to wade in patches of dense coral growth. Had he done so, he would surely have discovered that the coral is quite often not at all "like a Rock for thickness". Several times when I was walking waist-deep in water along the reef flats of the Barrier, I received a ducking as my foot crashed through thin upper layers into hidden cavities below. The bruises and scratches on my legs remained.for some weeks, and afterwards I always carried a stout pole with me to test the coral underfoot.

The construction of the reefs is not, therefore, as simple as Mr. Strachan would have had it. Reefs are created by many widely differing elements, including animals, plants and physical and chemical processes. Chief among the animals are the polyps that create coral limestone, but their work leaves gaps—as I had painfully discovered—that have to be filled. A great variety of other animals carry out this infilling process and they are joined by a variety of limestone-forming plants. Plants also have other important roles to play, binding the corals together, providing a top surface and even growing inside them. Superimposed on all these assorted organic activities are relentless physical and chemical processes. Some are obvious and forceful, such as the pounding surf that breaks off some parts of the reef, but rebuilds them by throwing them into new banks and shoals. But some inorganic processes, such as the chemical formation of the solid reef rock, are invisible and gradual.

As the builders of the greater part of the limestone framework, the coral polyps are the most important animals on the Reef. For so great a task, they are amazingly small. Their sack-like bodies, with a mouth at the top surrounded by a ring or rings of tentacles, usually measure only one-tenth to half an inch in length. By day most species are withdrawn inside their cup-like limestone casings; at night (when food is most often available) they extend their bodies and tentacles to eat and assume the delicate, blossom-like appearance that for centuries made naturalists assume they were flowers. It was not until the 18th Century that a French surgeon, Jean Andrew Peysonnel, and the Englishman, John Ellis, independently discovered that the polyps were in fact carnivores that lived on animal plankton, the minute organisms that live, and largely drift, within surface waters. Each polyp's tentacles shoot out minute stinging threads that paralyse and kill its prey, which they then usually convey to the mouth; where the tentacles are very small, this may be done by agitating fine hairs on the polyp's upper surfaces to set up water currents that draw a stream of animal plankton to the mouth continuously.

How these tiny creatures could construct the vast quantities of coral in the Great Barrier Reef and disseminate themselves over so great an area is a mystery that has puzzled generations of travellers. The answer lies in their reproductive techniques, of which they have two. To establish the basis of a new reef, they first employ the familiar sexual process of male fertilizing female. Then to build the limestone framework, they change to their second reproductive mechanism and bud asexually, splitting into two identical polyps, which then grow and bud in turn, and so on.

The first, sexually-caused stage of reef building occurs when existing polyps release millions of male spermatozoa into the water surrounding them. Some spermatozoa are drawn into other polyps; eggs produced there are fertilized and larvae duly develop and float away. These coral larvae, known as planulae, are tiny, pear-shaped organisms with a mouth at the wide, upper end and tiny hairs all over them which constantly beat and support them near the surface. Those planulae that are lucky enough to be missed by predators as they drift along settle on a suitable hard surface where the water is warm and attach themselves. They develop tentacles and gradually mature into adult polyps. At the same time they begin to secrete the skeleton.

When the first skeletons are built, the pioneering, sexually created polyps then multiply by the asexual method. They grow branches or buds that become daughter polyps, which then bud more daughters. This budding is a strange and fascinating process, but the majority of polyps are far too small for it to be followed by the naked eye. The mushroom coral, fungia, however, is an exception. To begin with it grows as a limestone stalk up to an inch high—comparatively easy to see. The budding begins when it develops a disc-shaped head reminiscent of a mushroom. The disc is a daughter polyp. It grows and creates its own limestone casing until it is large enough to face the hazards of an independent existence, whereupon it drops off and lands nearby. The beheaded stalk continues to sprout new heads one after another, until it dies. Meanwhile, the young polyps feed and grow into adults: brownish-green mushroom heads, some with long, waving tentacles, the majority with very short ones that rest, unattached and stalkless, on the sand. Some may reach seven inches across—the size of saucers—and are monsters by polyp standards.

In order to discover these extraordinary creatures and see the budding process for myself, I set out to the reef flats one day when the sun blazed from a clear sky with characteristic ferocity. As I waded out on to the flats, I could feel the sun burning my skin even through the shirt I had put on as a protection. Close to some likely looking coral clumps, I donned a diving mask and snorkel and lowered myself into the water, which was about four feet deep. As it closed over my hot back, quenching it so thoroughly it should have hissed, I left behind the unrelenting glare and bright reflections above and looked down through my mask into a cool, pale, dappled world of creamy coral sand cast into irregular dunes and ripples. Just to my right were a few lifeless-looking lumps of coral rock with seaweed sprouting from them

Looming over a jagged coral bed are contorted sheets of a purple echinophylliid coral (centre), each extending up to three feet across. Farther left are smaller colonies of lumpy-surfaced brown Echinopora lamellosa. The surrounding corals are species of acropora, whose branches may cover 75 per cent of a reef.

like weeds from a ruined castle. Pleasant, but strangely barren, it was not what the stories of multicoloured coral gardens had led me to expect. I swam towards the coral masses hoping for the first signs of the mushroom coral.

Some of the "rock" turned out to be living coral, including the radiating masses of blue coral *Heliopora coerulea*, whose skeleton retains its colour even after death. I swam up to the top of the colony, which was only a foot or so from the surface. Here everything was dead, and drab seaweeds coated the limestone. They had trapped minute particles of sediment, and looked dusty, abandoned. No sign of any fungia here. I stopped to examine one weed that looked like a miniature Christmas tree. Reaching out and expecting to find a firm plant I was surprised when it squashed into a soft, shapeless mass in my grasp. When I let go, the water buoyed up its delicate fronds and it became a Christmas tree once more.

Continuing my search, I swam to a nearby coral mass and clung to it to overcome my own buoyancy. A piece came away as I tugged my body closer, and the blue of the fragment showed that this rock, too, had been a living colony of heliopora. Seaweeds, debris and accumulations of small shells and dust had, with time, clogged the spaces between the plates of the living coral, and for some reason it had not been able to grow fast enough to avoid being stifled. It had succumbed and was now just a lifeless piece of the reef.

My luck here was better. Hauling myself along the rock on my arm, I found a crevice, and in it grew a little cluster of fungia discs on stalks, each disc half an inch to an inch and a half across. Adolescents, presumably. I touched one disc gently, and it instantly fell from its stalk deep into the coral crevice. Perhaps, like a ripe fruit, it was ready to fall, but equally I might have precipitated a premature "birth". I peered closer to see if the daughter polyp was showing any signs of survival, but it was lost in the microcosmic gloom of the sheltering nook. Instead, I examined the stalk. It was about two inches long, and had twisted itself through several right angles. Evidently the drifting planula from which it had originally grown had found protection deep down in the cavity, but the coral had been forced to accommodate several projections and obstacles by changing its growth direction. It now had the shape of a contorted worm.

The young fungia discs all seemed to have uneven shapes, presumably caused by obstacles restricting outward growth in certain directions. As I continued to swim round this particular mass of coral, my eyes became more practised and I began to find small fungia on stalks everywhere—beneath overhangs, in holes, lining cracks and other crevices and sometimes even standing, vulnerably, on bare rock. The emptiness of the sand seemed hostile compared with the comfort and interest afforded by the dead coral mass. Although adult fungia are normally found in the open and are quite able to cope with the hazards of an exposed existence, being capable of uncovering themselves after burial and even of righting themselves when turned over during storms, it was not hard to imagine that a secure foothold in a crack must provide a more reliable start to their life.

I remained absorbed for what seemed like hours until these very thoughts brought me to a sudden stop: I had not actually seen a single adult in all the time I had been swimming on this particular reef flat. I started looking for some, and after more than an hour turned up just two battered, dead ones half-buried in the sand. They looked more like fossils than anything living. Perhaps my particular set of adolescent fungia never grow up, retarded by something in the environment. Perhaps they all fall into their nursery cavities and never find their way on to the sand at all. Several, surely, must fall on to the sand? So why had I found only two? There is nothing that would be likely to eat them whole. And if the sand smothers them, I would have found more than two dead ones. I guessed that the reef currents there must be very vigorous on occasion, and sweep the adults away. Reefs have a habit of posing deceptively simple problems of this kind. I certainly never found the answer to this one, and nobody has been able to explain it to me either.

Nevertheless, I felt well satisfied to have seen budding in progress, for this is the method by which the framework of a reef is built. The large fungia polyps, admittedly, create only isolated pieces of limestone, in the shape of stalks and mushroom heads, which, as I had seen, can be swept away by the sea. But most normal-sized polyps join their limestone casings together to form colonies. To multiply and build in this fashion, the parent polyp grows a bud or branch that is an exact replica of itself. Instead of dropping off, however, the daughter polyp just moves slightly to one side and creates its limestone casing right there, in contact with its parent's. As the process continues, the colony takes on the familiar honeycomb appearance of a piece of coral, carrying out the process outlined by Mr. Strachan in 1704.

There are various advantages in this communal living, demonstrated by the different shapes that corals adopt. By being firmly cemented to the base on which they stand, colonial corals are much less likely to be dislodged or swept away than free-standing species like the *Fungia*. They are also able to raise themselves clear of clogging sediments on the sea floor. The staghorn coral acropora, for example, grows into antler-like branches so that the individual polyps are raised well clear of the sand. Millepora, on the other hand, grows into solid baffles that equip it to break the force of surging waves and flourish where other animals would be smashed to pieces. How corals came to evolve these shapes is a mystery that can only be solved by studying the genetic "programme" laid down in their cells and inherited by them from their forebears. Since knowledge of the inherited characteristics of any colonial animals, whether bees, ants or polyps, is sparse to say the least, the precise reason for the marvellous shapes of corals are likely to remain a secret of nature for a long time yet.

When many of these different shaped coral honeycombs "come to the full growth," as Mr. Strachan put it, they provide a framework for the reef, but at this point the simplistic view of reef building breaks down. Far from being "like a Rock for thickness," corals are often quite fragile, especially the fast growing types that might otherwise contribute most to the reef. The common staghorn branches, which may grow as much as two inches in a year, have only light porous structures. Brain corals are much stronger, but they often increase their bulbous girth by only a fifth of an inch in a year. Furthermore, all corals, light or heavy, are home for a multitude of boring organisms, from clams to sponges, and are soon weakened or broken by them. Before the corals can form a reef, they must be packed with filling material, provided chiefly by other reef organisms, and bound together often by encrusting, lime-secreting, marine plants.

The all-pervading infill is created as an end-product of the life and death of animals and plants. Fine sediment is created by a variety of animals as they bore into coral rock to seek protection. Other animals swallow sand and reduce it to finer sediment. And a host of reef animals and plants contribute their shells or skeletons when they die. Foraminifera, single-celled, shelled little beings, join the sediment in their millions, their ornate, often geometrical casings sometimes forming whole beaches on the Reef.

The cement for these building materials comes mostly from the limy skeletons of plants, which are indispensable reef builders. Plants grow around, between, on top of and even inside the polyps of corals. Sheet-like growths of stony algae, such as the delicate-pink *Lithothamnion*, cement together large coral skeletons and bind small bits of debris into hard clumps. Other algae infiltrate their filaments inside coral limestone, creating plant "mortar" that seals the gaps left by the polyps. Stony, red seaweeds grow on top of the corals where, unlike most coral polyps, they can endure strong surf. Indeed, they positively flourish in the nutrient-rich foam, and the top layer of many reefs does not consist of coral at all, but of hard masses of these "seaweeds". Considering the plants' contributions to reef-building, it is not surprising that early naturalists thought coral reefs were botanical creations.

In fact, scientific factions are still sparring with one another today over which are more important in reef-building, animals or plants. For there is one vital function fulfilled by plants that was discovered only early this century. The plants concerned are minute, single-celled algae known as zooxanthellae that exist in vast numbers in the tissues of all reef-building polyps—6,000 were once counted from a coral planula the size of a full stop. In experiments in which corals were deprived of their algae by placing them in a dark box, while providing all their other needs, the light-dependent plants died, and were actually expelled from the polyps, which then lost their colour. The polyps continued to live, but it was discovered in the 1960s that they grew very much more slowly—at as little as one-tenth their usual rate.

On a reef such slow growth would inhibit the corals from developing their characteristic and elaborate colony shapes—antlers, and so on—which in turn enable them to cope with the day-to-day matters of obtaining food and overcoming the hazards of their surroundings. Certain corals never contain zooxanthellae and they grow very much more slowly than the others. They rarely acquire the same kinds of large and complex colony forms and cannot build reefs. They are living proof of the importance to the Reef of corals containing zooxanthellae.

The first, most obvious function suggested for the growth-giving algae was that they provided food for the polyps. The corals were supposed to harvest their private crops of algae as and when they needed to. But if corals found algae so nutritious, then why did they never partake of the masses of related plankton plants drifting in the water all around them? To confirm the suspected relationship between zooxanthellae and free-swimming algae, some zooxanthellae were taken from corals and cultured into free-living forms. The polyps treated these drifting zooxanthellae with total indifference, and ate none, even failing to digest them when they were placed in the stomach cavity.

If the polyps do not eat the zooxanthellae, the algae must help in some more subtle way. They are, it turns out, rubbish collectors. Like all plants, they need carbon dioxide gas, since they use it, together with water and sunlight, to manufacture their own food of starch and sugars. Carbon dioxide is a natural product of the polyps' respiration, as of any other animal. Zooxanthellae use the polyps' exhalation to make their starch. But to build this starch into body protein the algae require other chemicals—nitrogen, phosphorus and sulphur—which, as it happens, are also contained in the unwanted by-products of the coral polyps' metabolism. Thus the algae, by so efficiently freeing the polyps of poisonous wastes, enable the corals to channel all their energy into building skeletons, and subsequently, reefs.

Nevertheless, these tiny algae impose limitations. Like all plants, they cannot live without light, and depth of water limits the amount of light that penetrates. Consequently, along the Barrier, and all reefs, the less light there is, the fewer and less functional are the algae inside the polyps. Coral growth is therefore slower and coral colonies become progressively smaller, until only the non-reef building corals, which grow without zooxanthellae, can survive. The actual depth at which reef-building corals peter out depends on how clear the water is, but dense coral growth is rarely found in waters deeper than 200 feet.

All the activity of plants and animals—polyps and stony seaweeds binding them together—take the reef to the last stage in its construction: the metamorphosis into reef rock, which really is "like a Rock for thickness". I once dug into the Reef expecting to find a mass of different fossil corals and shells, all cemented together but still individually identifiable. Instead, I was rewarded with a chunk of homogeneous creamy-brown limestone with nothing to suggest its animal and plant origins except holes and cavities. It looked rather like a piece of builder's rubble. The explanation for the change is really very simple. All limestone is slightly soluble in water, especially when under pressure. What happens on the Reef is that the comparatively unstable crystals of the shells and corals, constantly wet and under increasing pressure from new corals above, break down gradually into the more stable forms represented by the creamy-brown limestone. At last I began to disentangle the process that Mr. Strachan thought so simple, two and half centuries ago.

The processes that combine to form a reef operate wherever tempera-

The frond-like branches of a large, deep-water gorgonian or sea fan coral act as protective hosts to a clinging feather star (far left) and a brittle star, raising them free of sediment on the sea floor. At the fan's base a smaller, more fragile gorgonian coral grows up towards clear water.

ture, depth and ocean currents provide a hospitable environment. The strange thing is that much of the Great Barrier Reef appears not to have been hospitable for much of its history. In many places, its foundations are 100 fathoms down and occasionally much more. In 1959, when an oil company put down an exploratory bore-hole on Wreck Island, they found that it penetrated through 1,800 feet (the equivalent of 300 fathoms) of reef rock and debris before reaching a base of volcanic rock. By its own terms, the coral should never have grown at all.

The key to the mystery, and also the explanation for the Great Barrier Reef's geographical complexity, lies in a combination of changing sea levels and geology. Sea levels are seldom the same for long, and the Pacific Ocean reached its lowest point during the last phase of the Ice Age, over 10,000 years ago, dropping as much as 300 feet as water was drawn from the world's oceans to expand the giant polar ice caps. The shallower ocean allowed polyps to start building an extra 200 feet (or 30 fathoms) farther down, which explains at least partly why present foundations are so deep.

The base on which they built—the Queensland continental shelf—was far from flat. Far back in geological time, it had been broken by large fractures into a series of terraces running parallel to the coast and creating the impression of a flight of broad stairs, leading gently down from the shore then dropping quite abruptly to the depths of the Pacific. At right angles to these terraces were another series of faults, cutting across with deep grooves and clefts and dividing the stairs into numerous irregular steps. The picture was further complicated by erosion, which cut deeply into soft rocks and only superficially into harder types. In the end, a varied underwater landscape was created, complete with hills and valleys, ravines and basins.

When these were brought closer to the surface by the drop in sea level, the previous coral reefs were gradually left high and dry. Under the continuous attack of the waves, many of these old reefs broke up, filling the submarine valleys to great depths—certainly as much as the 1,800 feet reached by the oil company's drill and perhaps more. New corals, too, helped fill the valleys since, when they reached the surface of the water and were prevented from growing upwards any farther, they grew outwards instead and toppled into slightly deeper water. As this debris filled the next submarine valley, or step, it gradually raised a base that was close enough to shallow, sunlit water for more corals to start the reef-building process.

However, the jumbled pattern of parallel terraces split up by fractures was not destroyed, since the changes in sea level were not continuous on the way down or, later, on the way up, but moved in jerks and fluctuations, sometimes pausing at a particular level for thousands of years. During such pauses, the force of the waves cut more bold platforms and terraces into the older ones by means of erosion. So not only were the foundations of the Reef jumbled; they were jumbled differently at different times.

As a result of all these processes, both organic and inorganic, the Great Barrier Reef consists of a great many different types of reef; fringing, barrier, patch and ribbon reefs (but not the atoll reefs that support coral islands elsewhere in the Pacific).

A fringing reef grows up and out from a mainland shore or an island where the sea bed is often of a completely different rock type, such as granite. As the corals multiply over thousands of years, they coat the ancient continental rock with a layer of limestone.

A barrier reef is simply a fringing reef that has become separated from the shore. This occurs for two reasons. Corals are always moving out to sea because the water there is clear and contains more food and oxygen. Also as they topple over and fill up valleys ahead of them, they so to speak tumble down a flight of geological stairs, building up each step as they go. Second, a rise in sea level (or, in some cases, a gradual sinking of the land) causes the adjacent shore to be increasingly submerged and so to recede.

Patch reefs are formed on previously-established reef rock, where the water is shallow enough for corals to build—for instance, on the platforms and terraces of older, previously eroded reefs, or around islands formed by debris swept together by the waves. Growing straight from the seabed, with no hard rock shoreline to shape them, a patch reef adjusts its shape to the weather. The highest point is a bold reef front on the windward side, where the swell creates favourable growth conditions, and from here the reef slopes gently down into the lee. It grows at right angles to the wind, responding to the swell by elongating and presenting it the maximum area, and its ends sweep around in graceful, curving crescents. When such reefs become greatly elongated, they are known as ribbon reefs.

All these types of reef combined along the Australian coast create a massive breakwater, and it is this wall effect that gives the Great Barrier Reef its name rather than any technical definition of a barrier reef. In fact, the nearly continuous section in the north, where the trade winds blow constantly, is made of a series of ribbon reefs, and the various barrier reefs that do exist are smaller and mainly farther south. Where the prevailing winds are less consistent—in the south—some reefs sit across the line of the Barrier rather than along it. Where the temperature is lower and the water deeper, farther south still, the coral grows with less energy and variety, and fringing reefs and patch reefs alone break the force of the ocean.

In the shelter of reef crests, be they the bold fronts of patch reefs or the rims of barriers, reef flats form. These are shallow expanses of coral and plants, the gardens and deserts that contain a wide variety of the life of the Great Barrier Reef. Sometimes a reef flat can be particularly luxuriant: on two miles of the flat of one of the Murray Islands at the very tip of the northern Barrier, there were an estimated 3,600,000 clumps of coral. Even reef flats that seem to consist of dead, brownish coral covered in slimy seaweed teem with marine life: living shells, sponges, starfish, worms, crabs—and living coral.

Between the seaward reef and shore, at the centre of the reef flats, there is often a strip of calm water known as the lagoon or moat. It is generally barren because of its silty water. Nevertheless, its calmness makes it the ideal home for delicate, finely-branched corals, or those well-adapted to life on sand, like the mushroom corals. It is the supreme example of the ability of the corals and plants to create shelter. Just as the seabed made a home for the coral, so the coral makes a home for other life. Considering its importance, it is surprising that the coral constitutes only ten per cent of living matter on the Reef. The other 90 per cent consists of the fish, reptiles and creeping creatures inhabiting its pools, caves, flats and sand. In this underwater kingdom away from the force of the Pacific, they are free to adapt and diversify.

The Living Coral

PHOTOGRAPHS BY KEITH GILLETT

It is an astonishing fact that the 1,260 miles of the Great Barrier Reef have been built chiefly by animals only half an inch long: the coral polyps. They consist of nothing more than a sack of tissue with a ring of tentacles and a mouth at the top, but have the ability to secrete hard limestone casings, millions of which form the cores of the Barrier's various individual reefs.

The first unit of a reef is laid down when a larva drifts into a warm site well supplied with the plankton it eats, grows into a mature polyp and in the process builds up its case of limestone. It then grows a bud that is a perfect replica of itself. The bud draws away from its parent—without losing contact—and begins to operate in the same way, secreting its own casing to one side or the other. This process is repeated at an ever-increasing rate and produces an intimately united colony of hundreds of thousands of polyps. Other larvae may settle alongside, creating more colonies. After many thousands of years, their casings accumulate into spectacular reefs that are coated on top with a living layer of coral colonies, building still upon the remains of their forerunners.

The colonies feed at night, and then the surface of the Reef becomes a brightly-coloured, waving mass of stinging tentacles, ready to paralyse any tiny fish that touches them, and draw it into one of the many waiting mouths. By day, most species of coral polyp retract inside their casings, leaving a comparatively dull though fascinating variety of limestone shapes.

Not all corals build reefs. Some are too soft. Others grow too slowly to resist the battering of tide, surf and currents through their lack of a vital relationship with certain algae, known as zooxanthellae. Thousands of these microscopic, single-celled plants live inside the bodies of all reef-building polyps, aiding their growth in a way as yet uncertain: possibly they speed up the polyps' waste disposal and they may also provide their hosts with oxygen. Without them corals grow at one-tenth the speed and are unable to establish the framework of a reef.

These algae add an extra dimension to the extraordinary origins of the Reef. Not only did half-inch animals build a breakwater half the length of Australia: they could never have begun without the aid of plants invisible to the human eye.

The leathery folds of a soft coral colony (centre) contrast with the spiny skeletons of its reef-building relatives in the shallows around Green Island. The tiny animals—polyps—that built these structures are retracted inside them, awaiting darkness. Then they emerge and feed, covering the plain surfaces with a waving mass of coloured tentacles.

The interlocking "fingers" of the reef-builder Acropora hyacinthus form a pair of coral slabs each two feet wide and encrusted with other varieties.

The questing tentacles of tubastrea polyps unfold at nightfall as the colony, typically small and compact, prepares to feed.

The blunt rosettes of Goniopora tenuidens polyps emerge from their casing to feed. They are among the few corals to do so by day.

Viewed over a foreground of staghorn coral, the stony coral plates of montipora colonize the ledges of a tidal pool near Heron Island.

This mazework skeleton is a typical result of the reproduction of brain coral polyps.

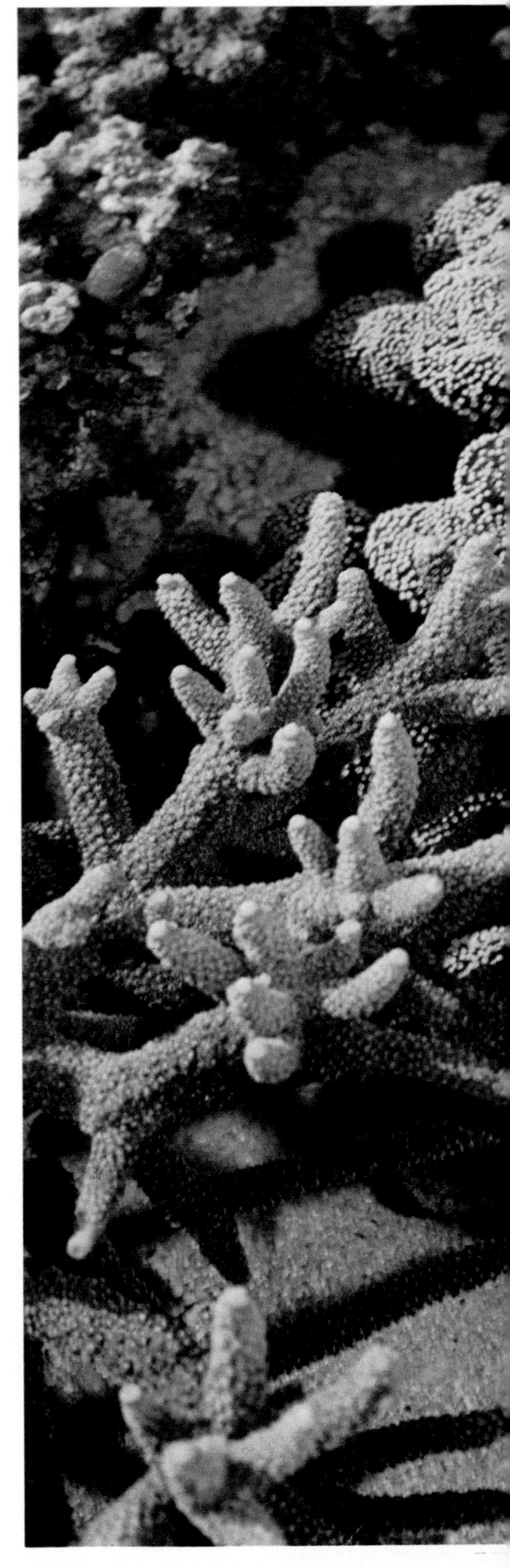

A stubble of half-extended polyps appears from the surface of the snake-like soft coral, Sarcophyton trocheliophorum, growing on the sea floor.

3/ The Many Worlds of the Fishes

Those myriads of fish created only to be devoured by their rapacious and insatiable enemies; enemies created in turn for no apparent purpose but to eat and be eaten.

ELLIOTT NAPIER/ *ON THE BARRIER REEF*

The afternoon wind rocked our small boat and waves chopped steadily against its side. A little way to the north-east lay Heron Island. A few fathoms below, lay three bommies, huge undersea coralheads that take their name from the Aborigine *bombora*, a submerged rock. Bommies, which are common on the Great Barrier Reef, are home to an incredible variety of fish, from bright little coral-pickers to the massive hunters that prey on them. Weighed down by a compressed air tank, encased in a rubber wet-suit, flippers and mask, I prepared to enter their world. A back-flip over the side of the boat, a rising shower of bubbles, and I was sinking slowly through the pale green. I arched forward and followed my companion, Walter Deas, downwards.

Despite the swell, the water was clear. As I dived deeper, kicking with my fins and intermittently equalizing the pressure in my ears, I found myself swallowed up in the silent world under the sea: the water pushed past my face, getting colder and colder as I descended; my hands, magnified through the mask's glass, seemed bloated and ghostly white, like a corpse's; the sea seemed to exert an invisible pressure against me, hindering my progress. It was like swimming against a heavy wind. About fifteen yards ahead, and twenty feet down, I could see the coralheads we were making for; the closest was shaped like the mushroom cloud of an atomic blast. The outlines were slightly blurred by the faint greenish tinge of water, but as I dived closer they became as clear-edged as if they had been in the open air, and I could see some large fish poking around the corner.

One of them came up to investigate me. It was a batfish: a large, flatsided fish shaped rather like a table-tennis bat, with a small mouth, grey stripes and an unquenchable curiosity. The batfish has one idiosyncracy: it often swims on its side, or at the diagonal, so that from above it can look almost like a plaice strayed into tropical waters. This one swam to within a few inches of me, peering straight in through the front of my mask. The others watched me approach, barely bothering to move, and swam lazily closer to the coralhead.

By now I was close enough to stretch out and touch the creased surface of the coral. It felt smooth and clammy. Lurking beneath its mushroom top were a dozen other fish, hovering close to one another: several big spotted cod, solid and squarish, stippled with bright blue freckles from gaping jaws to powerful tail-tip; and some black-and-white striped banner fish, each with its long topside fin trailing behind it like a streamer. Further down the coral face was a dark cavern. Swimming across to the entrance, I found a large coral "trout" inside with what seemed like a deformed mouth: above its actual mouth was a large protruding lip almost like the nose bump of a snapper. It stayed staring morosely at me, working its mouth upwards and downwards, and when I moved shrank deeper into the cave.

By now I was in deeper water, sinking slowly towards the ocean floor. Two separate shoals of tiny white fish, each less than an inch long, swam past, turning in the blink of an eyelid, the light glancing off the sides of their bodies; one moment they were dark and shadowed, the next they glinted iridescently like a flock of birds caught in a ray of brilliant sunlight.

There seemed a lot of small fish around that day; swimming forward over some beautifully shaped staghorn coral, I came across dozens of tiny sapphire-coloured fish darting in and out between the coral antlers. And a little later, near the second of the coralheads, I suddenly found myself swimming alongside the largest shoal of fish I had ever seen: they were almost as small as the first type, but this time there were thousands upon thousands of them, moving slowly past the bommie in an enormous, quivering stream, working their way forward *en masse* as though negotiating some unseen but intricate watery corridor. They swam in a strict yet constantly shifting formation; when I moved towards them they suddenly ascended steeply in one superb co-ordinated movement, an enormous mass moving as one, unfrightened and yet always just out of reach.

I turned from the bommies and swam several hundred yards to investigate the reef shelf that stretches in an unbroken expanse all the way to Heron Island; and now, for the first time, I came across one of the luxuriant coral gardens so typical of the Great Barrier Reef. It was a multicoloured extravagance of growth, and among the chasms and crevices of the coral bed there swam hundreds of multicoloured fish—striped, banded, finely-fronded, brilliant yellows and mauves and golds, polka-dotted and zebra-striped and piebald-dappled, luminescent and iridescent and densely opaque, deep black to veiled to transparent, snouted, finned, quilled and splinter-tailed—the glittering and fantastic creations of some child's imagination. They looked secure and peaceful in their watery dimension, and I felt very much an intruder, ill-suited to the world into which I had penetrated.

Here is one of the world's richest, most diverse and densely-packed marine environments. Over 1,400 species of fish have been recorded on the Great Barrier Reef but that figure seemed inadequate to account for the astonishing profusion and variety of life to be seen from the coral bommies, which, standing alone in deep water, were like some sentinels marking the border between two different zones of marine life.

In deeper water only a few yards from the coral, the fish had been comparatively plain, streamlined and mobile, patrolling ceaselessly in silvery shoals. Close to the bommies, however, the fish were brightly coloured, fantastically shaped and far less inclined to wander. The same was true in the coral gardens of the submerged reef. Here was a living reminder that the Great Barrier Reef is no more than a convenient label for a vast range of different habitats. These fall into four broad categories. First, wherever coral grows, be it a bommie, a tide-washed fringing reef or a submerged platform, similar conditions prevail, so the fish have much in common—notably the bright colours and extraordinary variety that first struck me. In a second category are all the shallow enclaves such as tidal lagoons with sandy bottoms, the mouths of estuaries and the no-man's-land of rocks, small sand patches, weeds and algae that occur at the edges of coral. Here fish move more slowly and take the colour of sand and mud. Third, in the deep and sheltered lagoon channel between shore and outer reef, roam shoals of the comparatively drab fish I had seen. These live independently of the coral, despite their proximity to it, feeding on each other and on the plankton in the upper layers of the water. Fourth, in the open sea beyond the

Striped catfish, wiggling the sensitive whiskers from which they take their name, swim in dense formation, searching for food in the shallow enclaves of lagoons and estuaries. They are well defended against predators, since each of their fins conceals an inch-long venomous spine; in shoals like this the concentration of vicious needles is almost impenetrable.

steep, surf-pounded ramparts of the outer Barrier live the ocean wanderers: migrating turtles, roaming sharks and streamlined shoals of blue-black and silver tuna.

The coral, more than any other habitat, provides the most varied living conditions, and therefore contains the greatest diversity of life. It affords shelter for animals including fish of all shapes and sizes. For the agile swimmers, there is a forest of coral branches through which to weave an escape; for the reticent, there is a cave or crevice in which to hide or sleep; for the predator, there is a grotto in which to lurk, ready for ambush. As a result, after thousands of years in which marine life has been able to adapt to these opportunities, the bommies, reefs and coral beds have become like a high-density urban housing development. Living space is so scarce that homes change hands at sundown. At dusk, the big-eyed night roamers—spiny squirrel-fish, the dainty red cardinals—leave their caves to feed along the edge of the reef. As they move out, the butterfly, angel and surgeon fish move in, replete after a day's foraging, and settle down for the night. Many of them change colour at night, becoming a toned-down version of their day-time brilliance that helps protect them against interruption.

Shelter alone cannot account for the diversity of coral life, which is also a reflection of the variety of the food available in and around the coral. The basic food is the plankton, a "soup" of microscopic plants and animals drifting in the sunlit layers of the ocean. In the constantly warm waters of the Great Barrier Reef, plankton reproduces itself at an astonishing rate. At night, it may make the waves lapping on an island shore glitter with phosphorescence, and light the wake of a passing boat with a bluish glow. By day, the plant plankton fixes the sun's energy, converting it into food for millions of minute fish, the fry of many species, which are such constant inhabitants of the plankton that they can be considered part of it. These, with other members of the animal plankton, are food for the larger animals, which in turn are eaten by still larger animals. For example, fish like herrings eat thousands of planktonic animals a day, a large mackerel takes 20 or 30 of these fish and a snapper takes five to ten mackerel. This eat-and-be-eaten process creates a food pyramid, with millions of planktonic organisms at the base and a few, large predators at the top.

There are many such food pyramids in the waters of the Great Barrier Reef, all starting with the plankton, and the most important pyramid in the coral habitat includes the coral itself. At night, the millions of coral polyps expand and extend their tentacles to feed on the animal plankton. The coral polyps in turn are eaten by a few fish that specialize in making meals of coral. Their shape and behaviour are strangely adapted for the purpose. Many butterfly fish have snouts shaped like elongated clippers and reach inside the coral skeleton and extract the polyps with almost mechanical precision.

Parrot fish lack such finesse. For a start, they are garishly coloured with reds, greens, yellows and blues. Then they have crude beaks, or what look like beaks and so give them their name. The beaks are in fact a set of fused teeth that constitute an immensely strong coral cruncher. Prepared in this manner, schools of these blunt, solid fish move through the coral colonies, browsing on even the hardest coral like a crowd of bullocks in pasture. The crunch as a parrot fish takes a mouthful can clearly be heard by a diver nearby. On one of my dives, I came across striking evidence of their appetites: a massive porites coralhead from which half the outer coating of living coral had been eaten away. It was like a cake from which a greedy child had stripped away half the icing.

The parrot fish possess in their throats further sets of teeth, flat ones that are used to powder the limestone and reach the live polyps and algae within it. The useless grit is then ejected. If a parrot fish is frightened so that it darts away, in its alarm it leaves a trail of miniature sand-bursts that sink to the bottom. Over thousands of years, this coral grit has helped to create beds of fine, white sand on the sea floor, swamping some of the coral growing there, while the reef above grows ever higher. Parrot fish move by day, feeding on the reef while it is light, but concealing themselves at nightfall in a close-fitting home crevice. Some species secrete a cocoon of slime that prevents discovery by scent-oriented night-time predators such as the dreaded moray eel.

The moray, which sometimes grows up to ten feet in length, is one of the largest predators of the coral habitat, and well able to consume medium-sized creatures like the parrot fish. When it does so, it indirectly consumes thousands of coral polyps, and millions of planktonic creatures. Wherever one looks, marine life starts in the plankton and ends in the jaws of the great predators.

The jaws of the moray eel are one of the greatest dangers of the Great Barrier Reef. Their knife-like teeth can inflict the most hideous lacerations, and although the morays are said to be unlikely to attack divers unless provoked, these powerful fish are renowned for their vice-like grip once they have taken hold. When driven off, they return to the attack again and again. They are constantly on the hunt. By night they are the terror of both night-feeding and sleeping fishes all over the reef; by day, the eels rest in coral caves, but even then they may lunge out to snatch at passing fish.

The morays have even developed an ingenious method of prising out prey that has taken refuge deep in a crevice. A triggerfish, for example, can jam itself almost immovably, deep in a coral crack, by means of a spine on its back. Undaunted, the moray inserts its narrow head and grips the victim tightly with its teeth. At the other end of its long, sinuous body, the eel throws its tail into a knot and then, with a rippling of slimy muscles, works it towards the head until it surrounds the outside of the hole. Thus braced against the coral, the eel pulls its head backwards and pushes forwards with the knot, rather like a man pulling a root from the ground by gripping with both hands and heaving between his braced feet.

The moray, though long, is dwarfed by the bulk of the groper, a member of the bass family and the reef's largest predator. Measuring up to ten feet in length it weighs as much as 600 pounds and has a disproportionately large mouth. There are stories of gropers swallowing divers whole. Experts discount these tales, but it is not hard to believe they are true when one sees a groper. The fish's hunting methods vary: it patrols all the coral areas, at one time lying in ambush in a cave, at another surging, jaws agape, across shallow coral gardens near the shore, engulfing everything that swims. Many other members of the bass family, though smaller, are also voracious hunters. With these, the gropers and the moray eels constantly on patrol, the coral "jungle" is an extremely dangerous place and all the fish that congregate there must look to their defences.

Some are armed; some, lacking their own weaponry, have gained protection from otherwise dangerous companions; others use mimicry to gain immunity from attack; nearly all covet a secure shelter, and compete fiercely for homes. These defensive adaptations are responsible for many of the bright colours so noticeable among the coral fishes, and for the behaviour patterns that go with them.

The angel fish, for example, use their brilliant appearance to advertize their possession of a daytime home and warn intruders to keep out. Any trespasser of the same species will be threatened by a twisting, turning display. The inhabitant's already bright colours intensify and its fins spread. It approaches the intruder, turning at the last moment

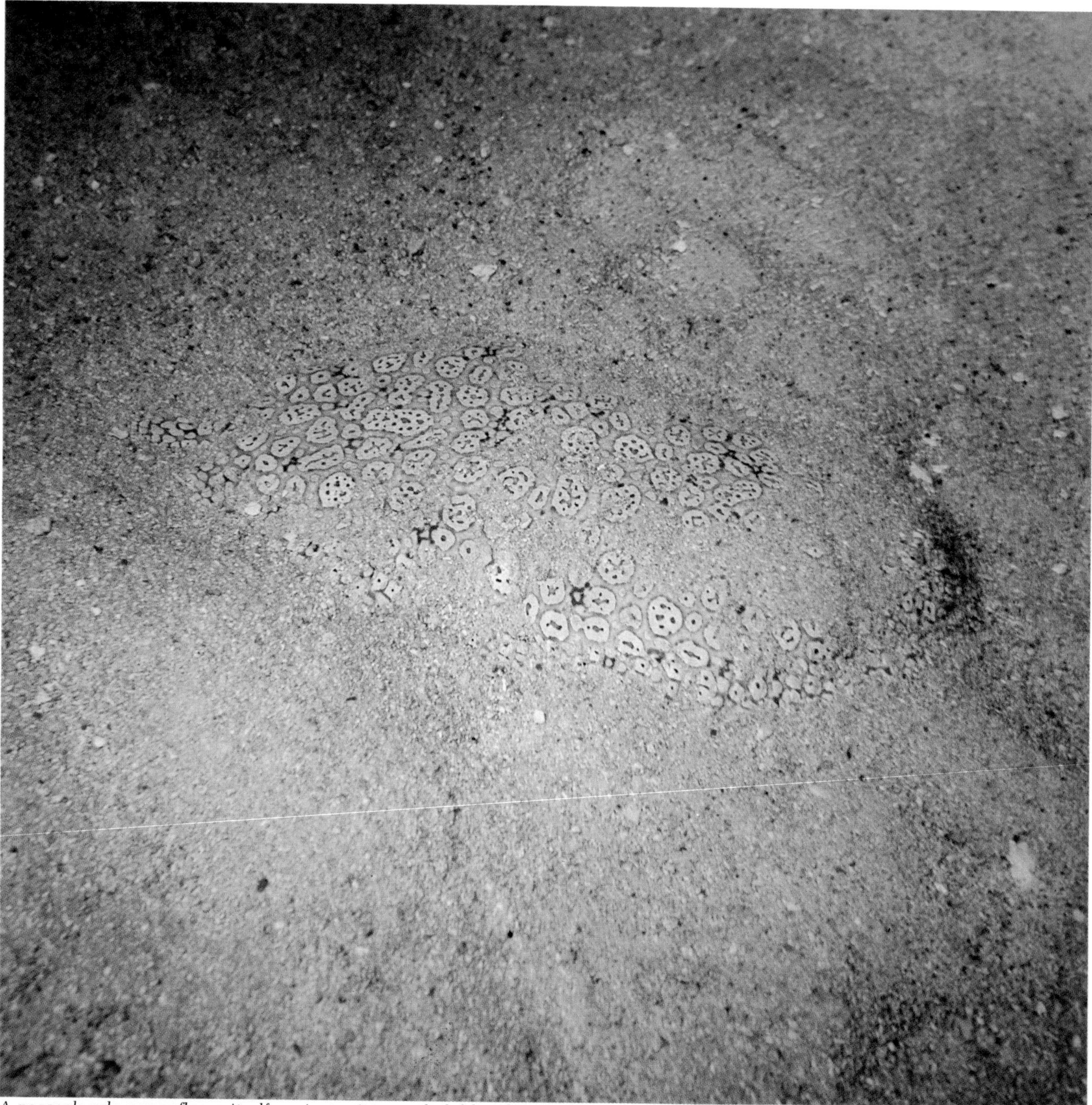

A peacock sole camouflages itself against gritty sand, deftly adjusting the colour of rings of cells in its skin to match the background.

to flash the markings on the flanks. If this show of colours is not warning enough, then a running fight ensues, as the fish spar back and forth across the borders. The most spectacular colours are usually warning signs to potential predators that the prey possess dangerous weaponry. The bright blue and white surgeon fish have spines as sharp as scalpels on their bellies, and the garishly striped dragon fish possess an armoury of poisonous spikes.

Another function of colour is to attract. The tiny cleaner fish use their unusual markings to catch the attention of larger fish, with which they enjoy a special relationship. One of this type, the blue wrasse, generally no more than four inches long, positions itself above a landmark, such as a tall coralhead, and dances and wriggles so that its distinctive black, longitudinal stripes and blue body create a flickering beacon of colour. This performance is quickly noticed by every fish in the neighbourhood, including the predators. However, cleaner fish are virtually immune to attack, since they offer the predators a vital service: cleaning their skin of the parasites common in these tropical waters. They also clean the edges of infected wounds. This servicing is an example of symbiosis, a mutual-help relationship between different species of animals. The tiny cleaners get regular meals (of parasites) and the large fish get regular groomings. The "customers" find the service so satisfactory that they will even solicit the attention of cleaners by hovering head-up in front of them with gill-covers puffed and fins fanned. They also open wide their jaws to give access to teeth and gills, and with sensible foresight refrain from snapping them shut. As a result, wrasse are prepared without apprehension to venture inside the mouths of even large rock cods and voracious moray eels.

This symbiotic relationship, facilitated by colour, is only one of many intimate liaisons in the crowded coral environment. Another of these is a shameless exploitation of the cleaner's role enacted by an unrelated blenny, the so-called false cleaner, whose colours are almost identical to those of the true cleaner. Blennies are small and usually shy fish creeping among boulders and coral crevices, but this one, *Dasson variabilis*, makes its living by performing a very fair imitation of the dance of a wrasse, even making sure there is one in the area to lend credence to its own presence. But, far from being a harmless parasite-picker, the blenny is a flesh-snatcher. Having tempted a victim within range, it darts forward, tears off a piece of fin or gill with scimitar-like front teeth, and dashes for cover, usually escaping scot-free: the speed of the blenny's attack and the shock it imparts are enough to protect it from immediate retaliation. Young fish fall victim to the blenny more readily than adults, which suggests that the older fish have learned to check a cleaner's identity at close range before accepting its ministrations.

A less predatory and rather more stable relationship is maintained by the clownfish. This little fish, brightly coloured in orange with black-edged stripes, lives among sea anemones, animals that look like flowers growing on coral rock, but have deadly stinging tentacles. The fish is thought to survive this flirtation with death by possessing a copious slime on its body, a substance that may inhibit the firing of the poisonous cells. Whatever the precise mechanism, it is an extremely effective way of avoiding predators, for few fish will follow the clownfish's headlong plunge into a dangerous nettlebed of anemones. Any that do will provide food for the anemone, and the clownfish will eat the scraps. Such free meals do not often come to the symbiotic pair, however, for the clownfish can be seen making dashing forays from its home to snatch small fish and shrimps. In such lean times, the anemone probably feeds at the edge of the fish's table.

Outside the coral environment, the pace of life is slower and techniques of hunting are different. In shallow enclaves of sand and mud and in lagoons and estuaries, small fish feed on debris among rocks, weeds and dead coral. Large fish feed on the small, not by giving chase, but by camouflaging themselves and lying in wait. Even some small sharks have adapted to this sedentary existence. The carpet shark, or wobbegong, is a good example. Gone is the familiar streamlined torpedo of the typical shark body: the carpet shark is blunt and wide-headed with a fringe of seaweed-like tentacles around the upper lip. Coloured, as its name suggests, like a grey and brown patterned rug, it merges with its background and, though it has been known to bite if trodden on, it is far from aggressive. To hunt, it merely waits, snatching passers-by with a short, swift lunge. Similarly, the pretty little epaulette shark, which gets its name from a pair of white-rimmed spots above the pectoral fins, idles around shallow water. Less elaborately camouflaged, and timid to a degree, it considers itself hidden if only its head is concealed, and becomes frantic if discovered.

Far more dangerous in shallow waters than any shark is the stonefish, a short, blunt, rock-shaped creature whose body is covered with warts, tubercles and weed-like fronds of flesh. Its camouflage is good enough to fool other animals and man, but in case of need it is armed with thirteen grooved spines that are sharp enough to penetrate rubber soles and can inject a poison that has often proved fatal to man. If it does not kill, it can inflict months of agony. The poison of the stonefish is purely defensive; it is the "insurance" against the attacks of other predators while it waits safely for its prey. When some small fish approaches, the stonefish opens its outsize mouth so suddenly that a miniature current is created. As the water rushes inwards, the prey is dragged with it. At one moment a tiny bream can be seen wandering among the rocks; in the next instant it has disappeared. The stonefish has had a meal.

In the calm lagoons, similar wait-and-see hunting methods are employed by many creatures. Since the water is clear and there are no caves or crevices in which fish can hide, predators must camouflage themselves on the sandy lagoon bed while they wait. The rays have adapted to these conditions with great sophistication. Their bodies have evolved into wide, flattened shapes suitable for hugging the bottom, with lateral tips that look like wings and give these creatures a bat-like appearance. They lie half-buried in the sand with only the eyes and breathing holes visible (when the tide goes down, tell-tale depressions in the sand show where the rays have been hiding). Although far from agile, they are nevertheless constantly ready to jerk forward with a swift flap of their "wings" and smother a small fish or shellfish.

The ray's defence is usually a sharp, poisonous spine at the base of the tail, brought into play with a violent sideways slash. It is capable of inflicting an excruciatingly painful, ragged tear in the flesh of an attacker. Some rays include electricity in their armoury, but whether for attack, for defence or even for some kind of sensing is not completely known. Converted muscles on each side of the head act as batteries, and can generate a powerful surge of electricity—up to 50 amperes at around 60 volts, enough to numb a limb or knock out a child and certainly enough to stun any small fish for prey. Certain freshwater fish generate electricity so as to produce a field of force around them that serves as a "sixth sense", a kind of radar to help detect movement around the fish. The electricity of electric rays may serve the same purpose, for such an ability would be useful in the lazy life of a lagoon or an estuary.

Lagoons are also the home base of sea snakes, the only reptiles apart from turtles that frequent the Great Barrier Reef. Large numbers of them can be seen basking at the surface on a calm, still day. They

While small fish swim by unharmed, a wobbegong or carpet shark waits in ambush, rock-like on the sea floor, for larger prey that will tempt its appetite. Unlike other sharks, the wobbegong is sedentary. It relies on its camouflage —including the seaweed-like fringe of skin around its mouth—to lie unnoticed by its victims until it snaps them up.

are considerably more active than the rays, and occasionally migrate vast distances out to sea. Usually, however, they move no farther than the coral and its borders, wriggling gracefully through shallow enclaves to flush out small crevice-dwellers, which they kill with their poisonous fangs. Although they are slower swimmers than many of the fish they prey upon, the sea snakes have a poison so deadly that once an unwary victim is struck it dies before it can dart away. The snakes are such certain hunters they sometimes leave the coral and venture into the lagoon channel between outer reefs and mainland, and harry the dense shoals of bream and anchovies to be found there.

In the lagoon channel, where there is no cover for isolated individuals, the shoal is the distinctive form of social organization for fish. Feeding off the plankton and small fry in the sunlit upper layers of the channel, the sea life finds safety in numbers, using many pairs of eyes to keep watch for predators. Huge shoals of herring, mackerel and mullet operate like marauding armies. Whenever they sight a food source, such as a concentration of fry, they charge straight into the midst of it, causing astonishing confusion. Fry scatter in all directions and many leap out of the water where they attract the shoals of the air, the seagulls. Up to 90 per cent of a shoal may fall victim to such a highly-organized attack. The same rules apply, one step up the food pyramid, to the sharks of the lagoon channel. The most common in the lagoon channel are the black-tip sharks, which harry the herrings, mackerel and mullet in large packs that present an awesome spectacle of savagery as they hurtle over submerged reefs during the chase.

To increase the safety of a shoal, the lagoon channel fish are conservatively coloured for mass camouflage. Gone are the spectacular hues of the coral fish, or the elaborate camouflage of the lagoons. The majority have blue to grey-black on their backs to merge with the dim depths when viewed from above, and silvery bellies to fade into the shimmering water surface when viewed from below. If a lagoon channel fish has bright colours, they are usually striped, so that within the group, the outline of each individual is lost and predators confused.

There are exceptions to the lagoon channel rule of shoaling: the slim, mean-jawed barracuda hunts in dozens rather than hundreds, like the shark, with which for ferocity it is often compared. It grows to a length of eight feet and has rows of long, sharp teeth set in an exceptionally deep jaw. Like sharks, also, barracudas often solve the problem of attacking scattered shoals by banding together and herding their prey into a tight coral corner where they can charge them as a mass.

As well as being highly efficient predators, barracudas have an evil though exaggerated reputation for attacks on bathers and spearfishermen whom they persistently "tail". The reputation is based on prejudices built up over centuries. In the 18th Century a French ichthyologist, Father Labat, propounded a theory that the barracudas hunt by smell and have a taste for man. He maintained that, faced with the choice of a Frenchman or an Englishman, the barracuda would invariably choose the Englishman. He reasoned that the gross meat-eating habits of the Englishman produced a stronger "exhalation" in the water than the exhudation of the Frenchman, who was a more delicate eater. However, it is now known that, unlike sharks, barracudas hunt by sight rather than smell. Apparently it is just insatiable curiosity that makes them follow human beings.

There is another fish that contravenes the lagoon channel rule of shoaling: the manta ray, largest of all rays, which lives generally alone. It feeds directly on plankton, and is so efficient a plankton-eater that it can reach weights up to four tons and widths of 20 feet from "wingtip" to "wingtip". It is often known as the devil fish, and I understood why when, on my very first dive near the bommies, one loomed up just above and behind me. Black and bizarre it glided past, flapping the tips of its wings in slow motion and waving its "horns", great segments of pectoral fins that flank the oval cavern of its mouth. As it slid past and disappeared into the gloom I tried to remind myself that I must have appeared as strange to the manta as the manta did to me. Pearl divers insist that devil rays will fold themselves around divers and squeeze them to death: but such stories are baseless. Deep-sea divers have died, though, when mantas fouled their air pipes or knocked hoses loose, perhaps in an attempt to rid themselves of parasites. Other mantas, caught up in mooring lines, have, in their haste to escape, towed small craft for miles and sometimes overturned them. Such accidents, however, are more the result of the size of the fish than of any form of aggression.

The true monsters of the Barrier Reef—the larger sharks—inhabit the open ocean beyond the outer reef, only occasionally venturing inshore. The five-foot black-tip shark of the lagoon channel is dwarfed by the savage white shark of the ocean, which can reach 35 feet. The largest shark of all—also the world's biggest fish—is the entirely harmless whale shark, seventy feet of dappled inoffensive plankton feeder, eating nothing more sizeable than tiny anchovies. It is the docile

A manta ray patrols the sea floor in search of food in this sequence, flapping its powerful 7-foot pectoral fins, then gliding and turning as it closes in on drifting marine organisms and small fish around a coralhead. As it sweeps towards a "landing" (bottom row), it closes its narrow feeding fins and guides the food-bearing water into its mouth. Two remora fish cling on, feeding on parasites embedded in its skin.

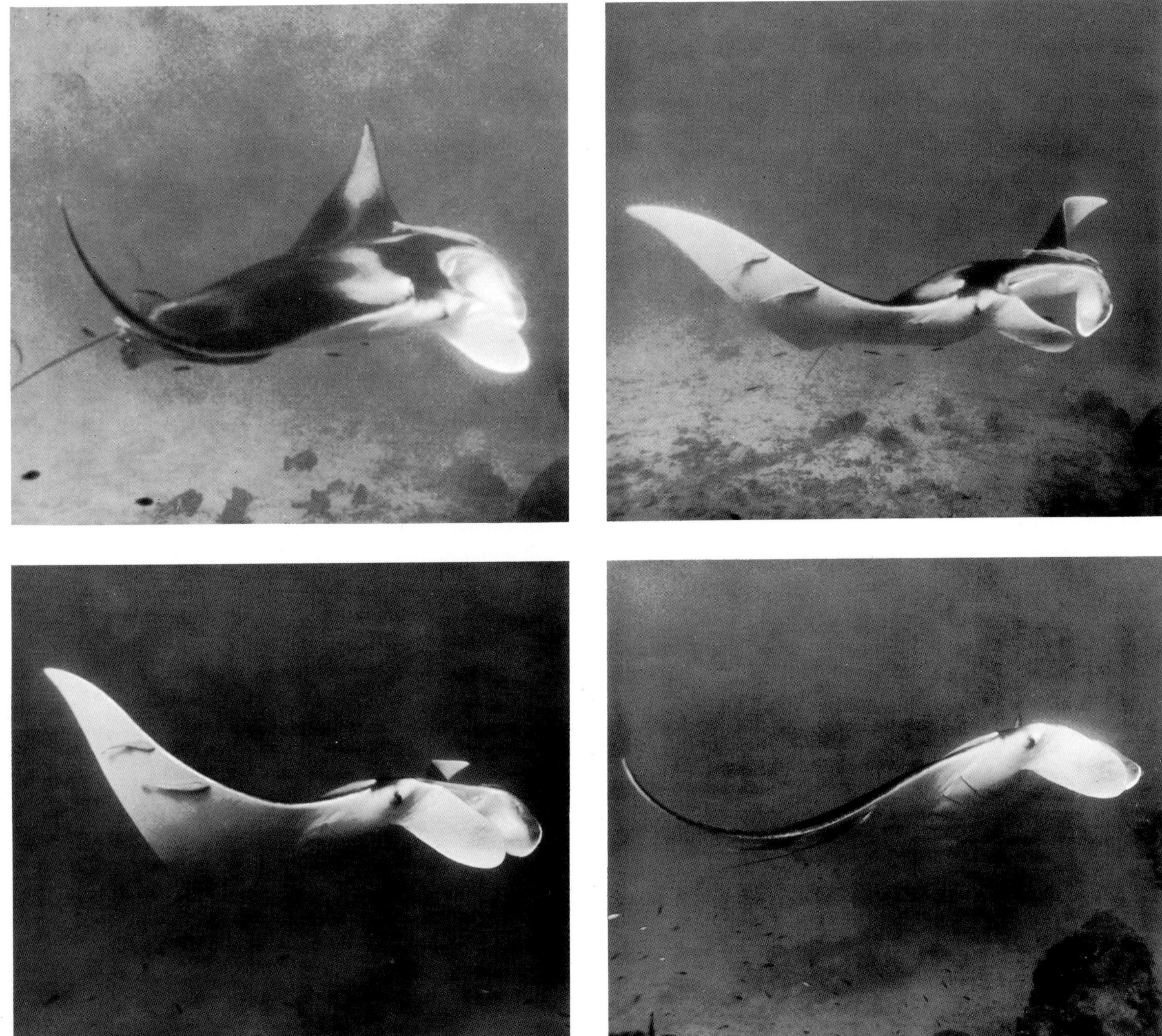

antithesis of its cousins, the notoriously vicious oceanic sharks.

All these big, predatory sharks quite justifiably inspire fear in seafarers the world over. They are armed with row upon row of sharp, replaceable teeth, hunt with a sense of smell so refined that over two-thirds of the brain is given over to its interpretation and are given to blind frenzies of feeding, when they snap at anything that moves. Predators like the hammerhead, its eyes set apart on the tip of its T-shaped head, and the thick-bodied whaler shark with its deep, jagged slash of a mouth are used to life at the very top of the food pyramid. They find their prey in large packets, hunting dolphins, porpoises, turtles and one another. It is hardly surprising that they sometimes attack bathers and small boats. But the world's most ferocious killer is probably the great white shark. Time and time again it has been implicated in attacks on people wherever they enter the open ocean. One study of shark attack in Australian waters, however, indicated that individual sharks, rather like rogue lions or tigers, acquire a taste for human flesh. This special appetite could result when injury or age slows the fish down, for man is easy prey.

Oddly, although sharks are superbly streamlined and efficient predators, they are actually primitive animals, hangovers from early forms of sea-life that have changed little over 300 million years, as their anatomy reveals. Like the skates and rays, their skeleton is made of cartilage not bone; they also lack the swim-bladder that keeps other fish bouyant, and must therefore move ceaselessly to avoid sinking. The fact that this primitive design has changed so little over so many millions of years is proof of its effectiveness.

The turtle, another primitive animal of the ocean, has a more chequered history. At some point in the age of reptiles, some 90 million years ago, an unknown change of climate or population pressure forced some species of land-living tortoise to return to the sea. Over the years their legs turned into paddles, their shells were lowered and streamlined, and they became sea creatures. Yet their origins have left them with a strange legacy. The females must return to land once every two or three years to lay eggs on the beach, and the shores of Great Barrier Reef islands are among their favourite sites for reproduction. I had long wanted to watch them arriving. To do so I had only to choose the season—December, which is summer on the Great Barrier Reef—establish myself near a coral island beach and wait patiently through the early hours of the morning.

Midnight: waves, glinting with intermittent flashes of phosphorescence, splashed gently on to the beach that surrounded the cay. It was almost high tide, and only a narrow band of sand separated the ocean from the dense, needle-strewn forest covering most of the island. Soon the turtles would come ashore. They make their vulnerable climb up the beach in the cover and cool of darkness, for they are easily frightened before they start to lay. They usually come at high tide, because then they can swim in over the surrounding reef, which at low tide forms an almost impassable barrier. At high tide, too, they do not have as wide a stretch of beach to cover before reaching the outer fringe of bush where they lay their eggs—and where I was waiting, thoroughly hidden by a screen of casuarina branches.

Even before high tide I noticed some dark, indistinct humps moving across the shallows towards the island. A little later the first turtle landed and began crawling laboriously up the sand. It was a green turtle, the commonest species on the Barrier Reef, so called because of its greenish mottled shell. For centuries it has been hunted for its tasty flesh and to make turtle soup, but it is now protected along the entire length of the Reef. It was a female, of course, and it was dragging itself forward with simultaneous heaves of the front flippers—a task analogous to rowing a boat across sand. In the darkness I could just make out that it was quite a big one: the biggest grow to five feet in length, and can weigh up to 300 pounds. It was obviously finding the trek up the beach an ordeal, and stopped every couple of minutes for a rest. Its hoarse panting came drifting across to me on the night air. When at last it reached the casuarina trees it changed direction and worked its way behind them, as though selecting a site. The first one, apparently, was unsatisfactory; after scooping up some of the sand with front flippers and flinging it backwards the turtle moved a couple of yards farther inland and closer to me and began scooping up the sand again, both front flippers working in unison.

For almost an hour this digging went on, the turtle slowly sinking deeper and deeper until the crater was about the same depth as its body. Then, using its short rear flippers, it dug a subsidiary hole about a foot deep in the moist sand at the bottom of the crater and inserted its stumpy tail. Before long the first eggs appeared, white and spongy and the size of golf balls. They came slowly at first, but then began appearing at the rate of one every few seconds. Green turtles lay anything from 50 to 200 eggs at a sitting, and may make six or seven laying visits to the same island during the breeding season, which lasts from October till May. While the female is actually laying the eggs it is virtually impossible to disturb; it almost seems to go into a trance, concentrating only on perpetuating the species. Then, like the turtle I was watching, it covers the eggs with sand pressed over with the hind flippers, and camouflages the nest still further by lurching around in the crater and throwing sand everywhere. Throughout the whole process, which takes two or three hours, this poorly-equipped, awkward-looking creature shifts almost a ton of sand. Finally, exhausted by the effort, it crawls out of its nest and makes its way painfully across the sand and back over the reef to the sea.

The eggs take two to three months to hatch. They are incubated by the warm sand, and when the young turtles hatch they have to fight their way up through more than a foot of sand before breaking into the open. Then begins the most hazardous part of the turtle's life-saga: the hatchlings, some two or three inches long, have to make their own way down to the protection of the sea. It is a deadly race, because along the beach predators wait for them: by day silver gulls swoop down upon the babies as they dash across the open sand towards the sea; by night the burrowing ghost crabs attack the swarms of hatchlings in an orgy of destruction, killing far more than they can possibly devour. Even when they reach the water the turtles are not safe: they fall prey to sharks, snappers, barracudas and other predators. Of the hundreds of eggs laid by a female turtle in one season, very few hatch into young that survive and reach maturity.

Very little else is known about the life cycle of the green turtle, though study programmes are under way on the Barrier Reef and elsewhere. Their migration routes, the distances they travel, their courtship behaviour and other details are still being studied. Mysteriously, very few young turtles are ever sighted in Barrier Reef waters. Even less is known about the other Barrier Reef turtles, like the loggerhead, which has a reputation for being aggressive and inflicting a painful bite with its beak-like mouth.

At daybreak, after watching several turtles dig and fill their nests, I walked along the beach to see if any of the creatures were still about. At the far end of the cay I found a young adult trapped on the edge of the bush. It had finished laying and was on its belly in the centre of the crater, front flippers flinging sand backwards like a clumsy breaststroke swimmer. In the daylight it seemed a cumbersome, prehistoric creature: ugly reptilian head, parrot's beak, mottled armoured shell hardly to be distinguished from the wrinkled hippopotamus skin. It was tired, and stopped almost every minute for a rest, panting loudly, neck drooping on to the ground. From one eye hung a large mucous teardrop covered in sand. Perhaps this was the first time the turtle had ever laid, and when it had at last covered the eggs to its satisfaction, its inexperience was revealed again. It heaved itself out of the hole and, instead of heading for the sea, made off in the opposite direction into the tangled bush.

That way meant death. Hundreds of yards from the sea, trapped in the undergrowth and fallen timber that litters the bush floor, it would inevitably perish as have so many other turtles that have lost their sense of direction and fought their way deeper and deeper into the centre of the cay. When it became clear it was trapped, and would never find its way out again, I tried to heave it round to face the sea, but it was too heavy for one man to move, let alone lift. An hour later I came back with a friend and between us we managed to swing the lost turtle round. Then began the long, agonizing descent down to the sea. The turtle stopped after very few lunges to rest, panting and sighing, the mucous tear swinging from its eye like a misplaced earring. It took almost half an hour for it to reach the water's edge. A final pause to gather strength, and then it moved forward, head submerging first, eyes still open, striving to reach a depth where the water would buoy up its tired body. At last it was afloat in the shallows. Its head went under still farther and only the hump of its shell was visible, moving slowly out through the ripples like a watersmoothed stone. Even then it did not make straight out to sea, but swam disconsolately along the shallows at the beach's edge. But then, as if its primeval instinct had at last reasserted itself, it swung towards the ocean and moved rapidly away. The hump disappeared. Suddenly the turtle re-surfaced, clambering awkwardly over some submerged coral; and then out of sight again. For a few moments the ripples of its wake remained; then nothing. For three more years the Pacific had swallowed it.

Nursery for Turtles

When the Great Barrier Reef's tropical summer begins, innumerable coral islands become nesting grounds for some of the most archaic of reptiles, the turtles. Like an invasion from prehistory, thousands of them arrive every year from faraway ocean feeding grounds, guided by stars and currents in a manner still unknown to science.

Some days after mating on the reef (opposite), each female leaves its partner to cruise safely at sea while it swims ashore and struggles up the beach to make a nest. With laborious care it chooses a nest site above the highest tides, where the sand is moist enough to make the sides of the nest-hole firm, yet warm enough to incubate the eggs.

The turtle digs in two stages. First, with powerful scything sweeps of its flippers, it digs a body pit deep and wide enough for all but the tip of the shell to be out of sight. Then, with precision amazing in such gross limbs, it scoops an egg-chamber two feet deep below its tail by alternate probes of the rear limbs. Resting often, it lays from 50 to 200 eggs, buries them and finally heaves and grunts its way back to the sea, exhausted.

After seven to ten weeks the untended eggs are ready to hatch. Individually, the young would stand little chance of getting safely out of the egg chamber: they weigh three-quarters of an ounce each and are buried under pounds of sand. Just before leaving the egg, however, they all become aware of one another's movements, and hatch and dig their way out as a team, usually in the cool of night.

They then have to race predators to the sea. Under the moon, silver gulls pace the beaches hungrily, ghost crabs hunt around the rocks and slower red-eyed crabs lie in wait for the tardy. Carnivorous fish from sharks to snappers wait in the water.

Large numbers of baby turtles never reach the sea, and the female has to offset these losses by coming ashore several times each season, laying up to 1,000 eggs in all. This increases the risk of being trapped on land and killed by heat-stroke in the sun. In addition, some turtles have been known to die in their body pits, apparently from heart attacks brought on by the hours of arduous digging and laying. These weaknesses on land make the turtle most vulnerable at the most critical stage of its life-cycle.

High and dry on a coral reef, a pair of green turtles mate, the male grasping for balance on its partner's domed shell. This seemingly precarious equilibrium is maintained by hook-like thumbs on the leading edges of its flippers, which are inserted under the front of the female shell.

A FEMALE GREEN TURTLE SWIMMING ASHORE TO NEST

EXCAVATING THE NEST

LAYING EGGS IN THE EGG CHAMBER

AFTER EGG-LAYING, THE RETURN TO THE SEA

PART OF THE BROOD DIGGING FREE OF THE SAND

FIRST TENTATIVE STROKES IN WATER

SMUG SILVER GULL WITH BABY GREEN TURTLE

4/ Coral Isles and Half-Drowned Peaks

There seemed the breadth of an ocean between us and . . .
those blurred and distant shapes.

FRANCIS RATCLIFFE/ *FLYING FOX AND DRIFTING SAND*

"The morning of the new life! A perfect combination of invigorating elements of the same, the sweet odours from the eucalypts and the dew-laden grass, the luminous purple of the islands to the south-east; the range of mountains to the west and north-west and our own fair tract —awaiting and inviting."

In these words, written in 1897, a Liverpool-born journalist, E. H. Banfield, celebrated the start of his life as a beachcomber on a coral-fringed Barrier Reef island, "wholly uninhabited, entirely free from the traces of the mauling paws of humanity". After years of fighting deadlines for Australian newspapers, he had built up so grave a case of nervous exhaustion that his doctor ordered him to abandon the profession and seek a more serene existence. Where better than on an island? He and his wife explored many of the hundreds that dapple the lagoon channel between the Barrier Reef and the Queensland coast, searching for the perfect retreat. They finally chose Dunk Island which lies a couple of miles from the mainland, south of Cairns, in roughly the same latitude as Fiji and Tahiti.

Dunk, the largest of a dramatically beautiful cluster called the Family Islands, is just one of the 400-odd isles that dot the long channel's 80,000 square miles of Reef-protected sea. With their coral gardens, wildlife and jungle vegetation, it is these cartographic pin-pricks, rather than the 1,260 mile breaker-swept coral barricade itself, that provide the popular, if romantic, image of the Great Barrier Reef.

Barrier Reef islands fall into two distinct groups: low-lying coral islands, or cays, that lie on the coral itself, and rugged continental islands that cluster in festoons near the Australian coast.

The cays are built by living corals working upwards from the smooth sea bottom. Once they break the surface as reeflets, sand and the debris of dead coral begin to accumulate and cling to them, often whipped into a crescent shape by prevailing easterly winds that throw coral debris into graceful, converging spits. At this stage, the new-born isles are little more than shallow sandy mounds, bare of trees or blooms, inhabited only by terns that brave the tropical gusts to lay their eggs.

Over the years, wind and weather transform them: sand consolidates into beachrock; shingle piles up, and, bit by bit seedlings take hold, swept in by breezes and currents or carried by birds. At last verdant forests appear at the centres of some of the cays—seldom more than 20 feet above sea level—and the islets become the foci of a complex variety of marine and island, animal and plant life. Many are surrounded by miniature coral reefs of their own, underwater except at low tide, and treacherous for the boatman.

The continental islands, made up largely of granite or other igneous rock and soaring to more than 3,000 feet, were once the peaks of mountains on the mainland; but they have long since been separated from the continental range, the intervening valleys drowned when the sea rose. Some have stark bluffs and headlines that clearly show their geological origin; many are partly edged around their coastlines with fringing coral reefs as well.

Their vegetation, sometimes reaching down to the water's edge, is like that of the mainland from which they have been isolated—jungle as intensely green as a Rousseau painting. Unlike many tropical forests, however, such as those of central Africa, and even some of the dense forests of temperate Europe and North America, the Australian bush is neither dark nor gloomy. The trees tend to have scantier foliage and the leaves tend to grow downwards (not horizontally, as is usual in Europe), and allow light to penetrate. These cloaks of green are usually heaviest on the western slopes. On the eastern shores the continuous bombardment of wind and spray from the Pacific tends to restrict plant life to small, stunted, twisted bushes and to erratic stands of trees that cling precariously to weather-stained jumbles of continental rock or shingle.

Many of the islands and the passages between them owe their initial discovery and their names to Captain James Cook, who sailed up the inside of the Reef in 1770. He entered the channel in the south where the waterway is 150 miles wide and the Reef peters out in a tangle of reeflets and labyrinthine passages. Most of the islands lie in clusters in the southern half of the channel and so much do they dominate the sea-ways that Cook was not even aware of the presence of the coral Reef itself until he had sailed 600 miles northwards and was trapped by the coral as it presses closer to the shore.

Moving through a constricted but beautiful sea lane, where a group of more than 70 continental islands, the Cumberlands, lie so close together that their spray-swept silhouettes are superimposed, he recorded: "... In the PM steer'd thro the passage ... formed by the Main-land on the West and by Islands on the East . . . everywhere a good anchorage; indeed the whole passage is one Continued safe Harbour, besides a Number of small Bays and Coves on each side, where ships might lay as it were in a Bason ... The land, both on the Main and Islands is Tolerably high, and distinguished by Hills and Vallies, which are diversified with Lawns that looked green and pleasant. This passage I have named Whitsunday's Passage, as it was discovered on the day the Church commemorates that Festival."

A shoot sprouting from a coconut on Dunk Island indicates how palm trees colonize Reef islands. The process begins when a fallen coconut is washed out to sea from elsewhere and carried by ocean currents to the island. In suitable conditions it is able to germinate, but it will take up to eight years to reach the size of this one and another nine months before it becomes firmly established as a fruit-bearing tree.

The Cumberlands are the most beautiful of all the off-shore islands. Some have the high, grassy, treeless slopes that Cook mentioned; others are rocky outcrops. Some are fairly low, sloping smoothly to soft beaches broken by tidal streams and enclosed inlets; still others, heavily timbered, rise steeply to over 1,000 feet. When seen from the shore, they seem suspended in deep aquamarine waters, but seen from a boat sailing among them, the water colour changes chameleon-like, from ultramarine to turquoise to rich sapphire. It can lighten to pastel green in the shallows or turn deep purple when monsoonal clouds shadow the surface.

A little farther north, Cook named the loftiest of all the continental islands Hinchinbrook, after the ancestral family seat of England's First Lord of the Admiralty, George Montague Dunk (near-by Dunk Island—on which Banfield later settled—he dubbed in honour of the First Lord himself who died the following year).

Hinchinbrook is separated from the mainland only by a tortuous passage, a drowned mountain fault; so closely does it hug the shore that its wild, craggy foliage-covered peaks, seem from a distance still to be part of the mainland. The late Professor F. Wood-Jones, a British authority on coral islands, used to tell of a hardened Australian traveller who once said to him, "No one can sail through Hinchinbrook Pass and not believe in God." The Barrier Reef Aborigines must have been similarly awed by the pass, for it was their belief that the 3,500-feet pinnacle was the lid to a chasm in which the winds and the rains were secured. They held that a malevolent devil lifted the lid from time to time to let storm and mist come roaring out, enveloping the slopes in terrifying purple clouds.

Beyond Hinchinbrook, the Great Barrier Reef presses closer and closer towards the shore. Cook, in his northward passage, recognized that the waters were becoming increasingly dangerous—but how dangerous he did not fully realize until, sailing through the dark of night where the main channel is less than 20 miles wide, *Endeavour* grounded and holed herself on what is now called Endeavour Reef. The explorer was among "rocks and shoals without number and no passage out to sea, but through winding channels . . . which could not be navigated without the last degree of difficulty and danger".

His ship repaired, he sailed on. And at last, from a steep hill on Lizard Island, 30 miles north of the present Cooktown, he saw the formidable line of the outer barrier itself: "I discovered a reef of rocks—extending in a line N.W. and S.E. farther than I could see, upon which the sea broke in a dreadful surf." But by then the island-studded passage seemed even more treacherous than the pounding breakers. He found a narrow, navigable opening into the Pacific—now known as Cook's Passage—and sailed precariously through it on the ebb. Two days later, the *Endeavour* was becalmed and was driven towards the outer barrier. He searched frantically for an opening that would carry him back inside. He spotted one, swept through it on the tide "as in a torrent", and, registering his relief, named it Providential Channel.

Modern vessels treat the dangers of the enclosed seaway with respect. Even small yachts, sailing locally amongst the islands and cays, are often equipped with echo-sounders, but the coral rises so sharply from the sea floor that the echo-sounder can be showing plenty of water beneath the stern, while the bow of the boat is nudging an island-reef.

Although some of the Great Barrier Reef islands have become popular tourist centres, many have been designated national parks and wildlife sanctuaries, and most are completely untouched. Stepping ashore on any that are uninhabited brings out the Robinson Crusoe in a man. It is easy for a visitor to imagine that he is the first person ever to land on the sandy beach, glistening under the tropical sun, perhaps with the trail of a goanna, the huge Australian lizard, leading up towards the trees as the only sign that some living creature has passed this way before.

Typical of such cays is One Tree Island in the Capricorn group. Only a few feet above sea level, with a couple of humps that reach up to 20 feet, it is a genuine, coral-built low islet—but with a difference. Perhaps because it lies on the eastern, or windward side of its own reef and is buffeted by Pacific wind and weather, it has virtually no sand, but is made up almost entirely of coral rubble. Shingle and boulders line the shore; its few groves of pandanus palms are scattered and wind-tossed; low bushes cling to bare ridges.

The island was named in 1843 by sailors on the survey ship, H.M.S. *Fly*, when they spotted what they thought was a single tree on the distant horizon. Drawing closer, they saw that it was not a lone tree, but as the ship's naturalist, J. B. Jukes, put it in a description of the island, "a small clump of the Pandanus of these seas, with its roots exposed above the ground".

In the centre of the island there is still "a small hole of salt water" that Jukes also described. It is a strange saucerful of liquid rimmed with grass so smooth that it looked newly born. The pond, a rare phenomenon on these usually porous islands, changes size from time to time but never drains away completely. Jukes also noticed a "large rude mass of old sticks" on the island's low crest—the roost of a pair of white-breasted sea eagles. It is still there, having survived the intervening century and a half. It is an impressive tower of dead sticks and branches, four or five feet across, and rising some ten feet above the ground in the shade of the pandanus trees. Eagles must have used the nest consistently, making necessary repairs from time to time, as any family in an inherited home must do; but for the last few years it has been unused. It has been preserved partly by sheltering pandanus palms, their trunks emerging from bizarre pyramids of pipelike roots that cling stubbornly to the coral rubble. I have seen pandanus trees bent almost horizontal from years of being lashed by heavy winds; yet the roots stand firm, even when the soil beneath has been almost entirely swept away.

Jukes was disappointed in One Tree Island, the first cay he had ever seen: "The whole was very different from my preconceived notions of a coral reef . . . It looked simply like a half drowned mass of dirty brown sandstone, on which a few stunted corals had taken root." But the island, with its bare stony ridges, windblown trees and dark boulders has a lonely desolate grandeur of its own.

For scenic grandeur of the sort Jukes was looking for one has to

The transformation of a bare coral cay into a wooded island begins with the germination of a few hardy plants, of which three types are shown here. Grass seeds borne by birds are usually the first to take root. Then come the water-borne seeds of goat's foot creeper (bottom). As these multiply, their roots bind the sand and their leaves produce humus, encouraging more choosy seeds to grow. Among these are the fan fern (top left), whose spores are wind-borne, and the bushy tournefortia (top right), whose seeds may be carried in driftwood.

FAN FERN

TOURNEFORTIA

GOAT'S FOOT CREEPER

turn to the offshore islands. Banfield's vivid description of Dunk in the first of his four amiable books written on and about his "delicious" retreat, *The Confessions of a Beachcomber*, captures the essence of one of these continental isles perfectly:

"Steep, forest-clad declivities, baby precipices of grey granite aureoled with orchids, tangled jungle from the splashline of the Pacific to the crest of the range; fantastic rocks, linked and corniced and skirted with oyster-masses; grey-fronded palms springing from clefts among austere boulders; grassy slopes, with groups of pandanus palms in steep hollows; and again forest and jumbles of rock, characterize the weather side. On the sheltered western aspect the less steep hills, wrapped in a patched but relentless mantle of leafage, rest upon a level plateau of about three hundred acres. This plateau has an elevation of from ten to eighty feet above a sandy, low-lying flat, drawn out into a western-pointing spit by the neverceasing action of the sea."

It was no wonder that one book reviewer, registering his approval in the words: "Almost it makes one wish to go a-Dunking!", crystallized a response that was echoed round the world. This was the time, at the end of the 19th Century, when the now more famous English writer, Robert Louis Stevenson, was himself "a-Dunking" in Samoa. (Interestingly, Banfield used the pen-name "Rob Krusoe" in an early newspaper article). *The Confessions*, in fact, inspired numerous victims of illusion from Britain who arrived, spellbound, on Dunk and some of the other islands and, fairly quickly, left. They departed not because the beauty of the landscape was lacking but because they were ill-fitted to the solitude and the self-discipline it demanded.

Although Dunk is no longer uninhabited as it was in Banfield's day—it is in fact popular with tourists—its natural tropical beauty remains intact. More than 6,000 acres are scrupulously protected and only 360 are in private hands. I could now understand why the beachcomber, who came at first for a temporary stay, remained for the rest of his life, a period of 25 years.

On a hot and breathless day in late December, I walked up and across Dunk, beginning at Brammo Bay, where Banfield had set up his first rough-hewn timber hut. From his "sandy, low-lying beach," I made my way inland past a thick fringe of coconut palms. The bush closed in around me, and I was soon climbing through a light-spattered jungle. Leafy branches soaring overhead formed an arched canopy. Vines and creepers looped and wound their way around tree trunks. Entangled ferns and other undergrowth made it impossible to move forward except by following a steeply winding path up the green-mantled mountainside.

The trees here, as on the other high islands, are mostly eucalypts, the ubiquitous gum trees of the Australian bush: huge blood-woods and iron barks with narrow, sickle-shaped leaves that hang downward, allowing the sun to slide and bounce on the forest floor.

In the centre there is a jungle of pisonia trees—tall, broad-trunked, with heavy roots as clumpish as feet. The pisonia's leaves gleam luxuriantly, and noddies nest amongst them. But the tree sometimes murders the very creatures that help it to spread. Its seed-vessels are covered with a sticky substance almost as viscous as bird lime; this clings to feet and feathers, and the seeds stick long enough to be dropped off or pecked off at one of the bird's next stopping places. But sometimes the glue is stronger than its carrier. Although large birds are not often trapped, when the seeds stick to the feathers of a small weak one, the bird may be killed as a growing layer of glue, seeds, leaves and twigs immobilizes the wings and encases the unfortunate bird until, as Banfield noted, "it is enclosed in a mass of vegetable debris as firmly as a mummy in its cloths".

Among the trees, I was assailed by the sickening smell of rotting mangoes; dozens of the yellowish tropical fruit lay half eaten on the forest floor, gnawed by some sharp toothed animal. I wondered what manner of creature it might have been, and later on I discovered. A frightening cacophany of whistles and shrieks came from the high boughs ahead of me—a weird demonic barrage of squeals that mounted to a sudden crescendo and then as suddenly died away. As I rounded a bend in the path, there, hanging upside down in the treetops 50 or 60 feet above the ground, were hundreds upon hundreds of "flying foxes", which are not foxes at all, of course, but fruit bats.

They dangle like thick clusters of ominous brown fruit, fighting, snarling, snapping at each other with tiny vicious teeth, gliding with barely a movement from one treetop to the next, their huge wings a ghostly transparent brown in the shifting sunlight. I began to realize why, throughout man's history, the bat has been a symbol of evil. The bats' unwholesome reputation seemed to make appropriate the stench of decay that pervades their feeding grounds. At dusk, they leave their daytime refuge deep in the forest and fly to the edge of the bay to feed on the mangoes and other fruits that grow wild in Eden-like profusion: bananas, paw-paws, raspberries and coconuts. The bats rarely consume whole pieces and much is left half-eaten, to rot.

I was now surrounded by—almost embedded within, it seemed—solid green: jade, emerald, viridian and chartreuse. Vines and creepers straggled down from the highest boughs, as thick as a man's leg, or groped their way up the tree trunks. Others created a dense, tangled barrier at ground level. The bush reverberated with sound: cheeps of insects; frogs booming singly from the swamp below; unseen cicadas setting up a sudden shrill, high-pitched drone; an occasional bird call; a whirr of pigeon's wings; the faint rustle of the wind—all the mysterious anonymous creakings and droppings and treadings characteristic of a tropical jungle.

After almost an hour of walking, I emerged into brighter surroundings. The path curved again to the west and levelled off. I had reached the summit of the tallest peak, Mount Koo-tal-oo, 890 feet high. There was no sense of climax: no rocks, no bare earth, no clearing—just trees and vines and a thick underfelt of leafy humus and dead branches.

Koo-tal-oo is an Aboriginal name, a testimonial, like the few mysterious terra-cotta paintings that have been discovered in caves, to the not-so-distant days when natives held sway over Dunk. Today, there are still a few Aborigines on the Reef. I could see through an opening in the trees, trailing hazily away to the south like blurred ships in a distant flotilla, some of the smaller Family Isles, also with Aboriginal names—Timana, Bedarra, Tool-Ghar, Coomboo, Budge-Joo.

After leaving the summit of Koo-tal-oo, I descended a steep bank lower down the mountainside and then crossed a creek choked with fallen trees, driftwood and waterlogged bushes. On the other side the jungle closed over me again. White cockatoos flew away with a weird unearthly screeching. (There have been about 15 or 20 on the island for as long as anyone knows.) Then I came across a more numerous but stranger bird. On a steep bluff above a harsh stony shoreline littered with black volcanic rocks, a scrub-fowl, a bird about the size of a largish turkey, native to many of the islands, suddenly scurried away, wings held high, half-running, half-flying through the trees, with a frightening gargling sound. I had stumbled upon its nest, a great mound of earth and leaf-mulch almost as high as a man, and perhaps ten or twelve feet wide. These nests serve as communal incubators for two or more pairs of birds. From a distance, they look merely like steeply banked parts of the forest floor. The soil of the mound is very soft, and a hen, digging her way in from the top, can be out of sight in five minutes. She lays her enormous eggs, covers them over, and then the heat of the mounds hatches them. The Aborigines regard the speckled, pinkish-brown eggs as delicacies, as indeed they do the scrub hens themselves, which taste like wild duck.

On my way back to Brammo Bay, in a forest profuse with garish hibiscus—huge saffron flowers with scarlet centres and stamens—I came upon some scratch marks on the flat ground. An echidna, or spiny-quilled ant-eater, Australia's version of the porcupine, had been rooting for ants. I was surprised by these marks, for mammals are rare on Great Barrier Reef islands. There are a few echidnas, the bats, a couple of species of rats, some wild pigs and little else.

At one time the islands supported a greater variety. Banfield recorded that there had apparently been wallabies on nearby Timana as late as the mid-19th Century. The last woman Aborigine on Dunk, who died in 1900, told Banfield about a wild and cruel wallaby hunt she took part in on Timana as a child. "Men, gins [females], piccaninnies," he quoted her as saying, "shouting, yelling and screaming, and clashing nulla-nullas (throwing-sticks), supported by barking and yelping dogs, swept the timid wallabies up through the tangle of jungle, until like the Gadarene swine they ran, or rather hopped, down a steep place into the sea, or fell on fatal rocks laid bare below by the ebb-tide."

I made my way through a grove of trees to the cairn where the beachcomber and his wife lie buried in the Banfield Memorial Cemetery. A few gaudy hibiscus sprouted in the jungle behind it. Leaves moved quietly in a gentle breeze. I read the inscription, the words of the American naturalist-philosopher, Henry Thoreau, another who turned his back on civilization: "If a man does not keep pace with his companions, perhaps it is because he hears a different drummer. Let him step to the music which he hears."

NATURE WALK / Island Forest to Ocean Edge

PHOTOGRAPHS BY WALTER DEAS

Heron Island, like most coral cays, supports an extraordinary variety of Great Barrier Reef life, even though it is only just over 40 acres in area and less than 300 yards wide. One summer's day, the photographer, Walter Deas, and I walked across Heron to study the creatures that live upon it and in the surrounding waters. We began at Shark Bay on the eastern end. The sand here, only a few yards wide, slopes rapidly, interrupted by scattered strips of beachrock, the only "rock" found on coral cays. Formed from cemented sand and debris, it is hard and jagged close to the sea, but so friable further up the beach that it breaks off in one's hand.

The sea was a flat, shining, almost translucent green interspersed with dark blue splotches where the coral lay just beneath the surface. It was an hour to low tide, and soon knotty clumps would appear above the ebbing water. It was peaceful. White-capped noddy terns and black-capped terns wheeled above the reef flat, occasionally plummeting headfirst into the sea for fish. Along the narrow strand, stilt-legged waders strutted, heads tilted forward, long curved bills jabbing at the sand: pick, pick, pick. A flock of crested terns and two seagulls stood motionless at the water's edge, basking in the sun. Heron Island at midday. Stasis.

We made our way up the beach to the perimeter of the dense bush that covers the island's centre. At the outer edge stood a grove of pandanus palms, perched awkwardly on the strange clothes-prop roots that enable the trees to live when the beds of sand are washed or blown away from beneath them.

Exploding Pandanus Seeds

The ground was heavily strewn with dead pandanus fronds, intertwined like a roughly-woven native mat. Beneath one tree lay a cluster of bright orange nuts, the seeds of the pandanus. They are contained in fruit about the size of pineapples and called breadfruit by the Aborigines, who grind the nuts to produce a coarse flour. At first the breadfruit are almost the same greeny-yellow colour as pineapples, but as they ripen they turn the bright orange of paw-paws. When they reach maturity they explode, shooting their nuts in every direction. Sometimes, on a still night, you can hear the eerie "bang" as they suddenly disintegrate.

Stooping to walk beneath a low

PANDANUS PALMS

bough that seemed almost an entrance into the bush, we found ourselves among the dense pisonias of which most of the forest consists. Pisonias, large and pale, with broad tropical leaves, grow to 50 feet and provide branching shade from the tropical sun. But the cyclones that often roar through the Great Barrier Reef in high summer batter these tall but brittle trees furiously and sometimes uproot them: the forest floor is littered with broken branches and tangled roots.

Perched high in the topmost branches of a pisonia tree was a long-legged, long-beaked, white heron, the bird that gives the island its name. Shoulders hunched, neck tensed, it watched us warily. As we moved closer, trying to get a better view, it took flight, feet together, neck outstretched, massive wings beating through the treetops, uttering a series of harsh squawks. Then we spotted the heron's nest on a branch just slightly above us. These nests, rough bundles of twigs, are fairly easy to detect if one knows where to look for them; this was the first time I had ever seen one so low. Two fluffy bundles of feathers peered down at us from over the nest's edge. No wonder the adult heron had been so upset at our arrival.

WHITE HERON CHICKS

I scaled the sloping tree trunk to look at the chicks more closely. They were both pale grey, with bright orange beaks and incongruous green legs. One, slightly older and a little larger than the other, had a greenish tinge to its feathers.

They seemed cautious, but unafraid. The younger one walked around the rough nest yawning, its furry topknot rippling in the breeze, while the older one studied me in absolute silence. I watched them for a while, hoping the adult bird—no doubt the mother—might return.

But my presence probably prevented that, so I climbed back down.

On the ground below, we found a single, broken, pale-green eggshell from which one of the chicks had probably hatched. Nearby lay two heron feathers: one large and white, obviously from an adult bird, and the other soft and downy, a bit of fluff from one of the chicks.

As we walked along, the pisonias gave way briefly to a clump of tournefortia trees, also typical on these coral cays. Much smaller than pisonias, they have soft green leaves and curling tendrils from which tiny white flowers sprout. Their branches grow upward and outward in graceful sweeping curves like multipronged candelabra.

Now we decided to strike out to the south, through a section of the island unknown to me. Almost at once, we were in a wilderness of dead brambles, with only here and there an isolated pisonia. We seemed to have blundered into an apparently decadent part of the forest. Suddenly I felt a sharp sting in my arm, as if it had been jabbed by a red-hot needle. I cursed, and turned in time to see a large insect buzzing away through the bush. A wasp? In a few seconds it alighted on a saucer-shaped honeycomb, a nest baked as dry as white clay, built in a tangle of dead brambles. It was a wasp; a few others clung to the comb, occasionally making forays in search of nectar.

TWISTED TOURNEFORTIA TREES

WASP NEST

Soon we were again in a dense growth of pisonias. Near their roots were a number of small, sandy burrows that looked as though they had been dug by rabbits. But these are the homes of the wedge-tailed shearwater or mutton bird—so called because early settlers thought its oily flesh tasted like mutton. It is one of the many migratory species that stop over in the Barrier Reef islands to breed.

I bent down to examine a burrow. Its entrance, protected by dead twigs and faded yellow leaves, seemed barely wide enough to permit a bird to enter. But underground, it became much broader, and it extended back so far that I could not touch the end. There were neither birds nor eggs inside. Sometimes one of a pair stays in the burrow all day, while its mate goes out to sea to feed. But their laying season had not yet begun, so both male and female were free to come and go as they pleased.

Thousands of Noddy Terns

The muffled drone of the surf breaking on the outer reef was now far behind us. We were overwhelmed by a new sound: the caws and cries of thousands of noddy terns, smallish black seabirds with white-grey headcaps. Their nests, shabby, unimpressive bundles of dead brown pisonia leaves glued together with bird excreta, were plumped on the pisonia boughs, with bits and pieces drooping over the sides.

The noddies seem utterly unafraid of people. One swooped up for a closer look at us, flew in a tight circle and then alighted a few inches away at eye level. It stood in an

MUTTON BIRD'S BURROW

ungainly fashion on its large, paddle-like, webbed feet, stretching its neck forward as though to keep its balance. Noddies are more at home at sea: you often see great flocks of them miles from land, skimming the ocean surface and occasionally diving down to swoop on small fish.

Every time we moved a few steps, or there was an unexpected sound—the silver gonging of a peewee, perhaps—the noddies set up a fresh tumult of noise, their harsh crow-like screams swelling to a bizarre crescendo. Suddenly a number of them began to flap around our heads. I wondered why. I got my answer in a moment when one, sitting on a nest nearby, shifted slightly to reveal a glimpse of an egg. So the noddies were already laying here. They certainly were not laying elsewhere. I looked further, and found that nearly every nest in the tree contained an egg, light brown, mottled with dark brown spots.

This explained an incident of the day before, when the noddies had attacked a white heron that settled on a tree near them. Herons sometimes eat noddy eggs, though they prefer to fish in the shallows.

The heron had beaten the noddies off, and then, as if to emphasize its superiority, walked over to a nesting noddy, grabbed its beak in its own much larger one and forced the bird backwards off the bough. But that nest must have been empty, because, having achieved its victory, the heron merely sat by the nest smugly, while the noddies squawked intermittently.

At last, open ground; but only

WHITE-CAPPED NODDY TERN

NODDY TERN'S EGG

for a few yards. Then the forest—now a briary bush—closed in again. We pushed our way through dense thickets of wedelia, a bramble-like shrub with a dainty, daisy-like flower. It flourishes luxuriantly on coral cays, as do several other bushes: the waxy-leafed scaevola and the exotic euphorbia, or flame-leaf, with its deep pink flowers.

There was little more to see here, so we turned and struck out for the beach that runs along the northern end of the island and fronts one of the richest sections of the surrounding reef. As we walked back through groves of pisonia trees and pandanus palms, the sound of the surf breaking on the reef gradually became louder, and at last we caught a glimpse of white sand through the undergrowth.

The beach here is fringed with casuarinas, beautiful, graceful trees that droop like willows and carpet the sand with thin, delicate leaves, almost as finc as pine needles. Thanks to these leaves, which allow little evaporation in the tropical sun and are resistant to salt spray, the casuarina can live even closer to the water than the pandanus.

A few more yards and, brushing past the casuarinas' low-hanging boughs, we broke through on to the beach itself. It was now almost low tide, and the reef looked like a boulder-strewn mudflat. Unprepossessing lumps of what appeared to be dead coral protruded above the sea. The water, with the tide ebbing, was already so low that it barely covered the acres of reef around the island. In the distance, perhaps half a mile offshore, a thin white line of surf marked the outer edge of the reef. As the tide withdrew even further, more and more of the disfigured, dark brown coral emerged, until the entire sweep between shore and reef-edge appeared utterly barren and without movement. Looking at it, it seemed impossible that any life could possibly exist there.

CASUARINA TREES ON THE BEACH

The Living Sea

I was wrong. As we waded out across the sand, through water which was at first ankle-deep and then knee-deep, I began to realize that, although much of the coral that is exposed above the water is, in fact, dead, it harbours a surprising range of sea life. Soon we encountered our first undersea creature—a brown mottled starfish, one of the commonest inhabitants of the reef that surrounds Heron Island. Shoals of tiny transparent fish, scarcely an inch long, darted through the glassy shallows ahead of us, almost invisible against the sandy seabed.

Then we began coming across another reef denizen, the bêche-de-mer, also known as the trepang or the sea cucumber. Dozens lay on the sea floor, each about a foot long and curled into a part-circle, like so many sausages in a delicatessen. Most were black or dappled black-and-white. One was feeding on the sandy floor. Because they

CORAL REEF FLAT AT LOW TIDE

actually eat the sand, extracting minute nourishment from it, they have still another name: the vacuum cleaners of the sea. I picked one up: it was like a large loaf of bread, light and spongy. It began at once to extrude white sticky threads—its weapon against enemies. The adhesive stringy stuff clung to its own body, and it soon looked as though it were in a partially spun cocoon.

Unexpectedly, for they usually feed on seaweed of which there was none to be seen, we saw a sea-hare, an ugly, wart-covered, pea-green monster, about three inches long. It was crawling laboriously over the coral, its four stubby feelers protruding from the front of its head, reminiscent more of a slug than a hare. Unlike a slug, however, it has three inter-connecting stomachs which

SEA HARE'S INK SCREEN

progressively shred the seaweed into finer and finer fragments.

When I touched it, it suddenly ejected out of its backside a dye as deep red as cochineal. The water for four or five feet around was stained at once, and whorls and loops of intense carmine red drifted away in the current. A second touch, and it ejected even more of the defensive dye. This seemed to annoy a purple-lipped clam nearby: for it closed itself and spouted a jet of water high into the air. A few seconds later, as the sea hare's dye drifted over it again, another geyser of water shot up from the clam. The spouting looked like an attempt at retaliation. It was not: clams spout as a matter of course to get rid of matter they cannot digest. One sometimes sees their jets breaking the

CORAL CLUMP

surface of the water one after another, as though a miniature school of whales were at play.

By that time, we had reached the first submerged reefs of coral, and were having to pick our way between them. Some were only the size of cauliflowers; but others were large disc-shaped conformations, gnarled by irregular outcroppings and covered with brown algae, deep-green turtle grass and sea shells: a drab scene compared with the fantastic variety of colours and shapes that exist beneath the deep water of the outer reef.

The water here was absolutely colourless; and only an occasional ripple marred the calm unruffled surface, betraying the current that swirls around the island. It was a still, brilliant day: shifting light patterns glinted on the smooth sea, fragmenting and splintering like stroboscopic lights at a pop concert. I could hear the raucous cries of seabirds, and, looking back towards the shore, I could see them, black dots wheeling above the beachside fringe of trees. The breeze was little more than a rustle. The sea and its teeming life were absolutely silent, except for the monotonous drone of the surf breaking on the outer reef, so faint that it seemed something I heard only in my mind.

On the Reef Platform

The coral was becoming so dense that it was no longer possible to pick our way between it. Instead we stepped up on to the coral platform and began to walk across the top. The reef here forms a stable floor, but there is a slight risk of crashing through a fragile section. Moving gingerly forward, we saw a number of clams with their shells open. Most were less than a foot wide, smaller brothers to the giant clams that live farther north in the Great Barrier Reef. They had beautifully coloured lips—some green and black like gaudy carpet snakes, others variegated shades of purple, mauve and brown.

Near a great long trail of *Caulerpa racemosa*, a green seaweed with bulbous protuberances that look like tiny bunches of grapes, were some tiger cowries, their shells beautifully marked and highly polished.

We were now about half a mile from the island, approaching the outer crest of the reef, and the coral had become much more densely

CAULERPA RACEMOSA SEAWEED

TIGER COWRIE

LINCKIA LAEVIGATA, A BLUE STAR-FISH

FEATHER-STARS

packed. I no longer had the sensation of walking precariously on the brittle ceiling of an undersea cavern. I felt now that I was on solid, dependable rock. The reef was strewn with rubble—bits of broken coral, shells and skeletons. Digging into it with my hands, I was unable to break through into any hollow underneath.

Life here is much more abundant than it is closer to shore. In rapid succession, we saw crabs of all sizes, more bêches-de-mer and starfish. One in particular stood out; it was a rich royal blue, dramatically beautiful, with its arms stretched against a background of almost pure white. Not far away were some feather-stars, their delicate frond-like arms rippling gracefully in rhythm with the gentle undulations of the placid sea.

TENTACLES AND MOUTH OF FUNGIA CORAL

Then came a green coral, shaped rather like a bun. Its polyps were extended—a most uncommon sight in the daytime—and they too waved freely in the current. I touched them lightly, and those closest to my finger withdrew. But the others remained extended; it was only when I pressed really hard against them that they all disappeared, revealing the coral's skeleton with its intricate pattern of interlocked honeycombs. I stood there for a few minutes, marvelling that such tiny, shy creatures—green and blue and pink and grey, slowly building living structures shaped like leaves and flowers and fans and fluted mushrooms—could have built the immense natural structure of the reef, a unique wilderness for so much sea life.

More and more of the patient reef-builders appeared before us—

first a heart-shaped coral, then a great field of staghorn coral. Their spiky branches shot off in a dozen directions. Myriads of tiny fish flashed and darted among them.

We had seen fish all along our walk, disappearing as if by magic when we splashed towards them. But now there seemed to be hundreds—brilliantly coloured, dancing and swerving, diving under overhanging coral at the first sight of an intruder, then emerging again if you waited patiently. Bright yellow, green and purple, they flashed in front of us. One that was tiny and almost translucent popped into a crevice in the reef as we moved towards it. The only fish that did not dash off in search of cover was a box-fish—a sort of swimming matchbox with snout, tail and yellow fins. It swam on unconcernedly in front of us, though always just far enough away to be safely out of reach.

Now the water was colder. Ahead there was a distinct line, beyond which it became a vivid green. This marked the edge of the coral shelf where it drops 40 feet down a steep cliff to a deep-water channel. Off to the right, white breakers curled and foamed over the reef's outer extremity. As we walked on, I could feel the shallow waves begin to lap at my legs in quick succession, one wave every two or three seconds.

A frightened green turtle splashed off through the shallows urgently churning the surface, like an old-fashioned paddle-wheel steamer.

The water had deepened rapidly and was now almost waist-high. It had begun to foam and bubble so much that it was impossible any longer to see the reef floor; walking was becoming dangerous. The dark green of the deep-water channel was now only three or four yards ahead. Then there was a faint line of coral, the outer rampart, and beyond that, the dense blue of the Pacific Ocean.

It was getting late but I was reluctant to leave before completing my exploration with a dive. Walter's wife picked us up in their launch and we circled round to the other side of the island. Approaching warily, we anchored at a point from which we could swim back in over the western coral fields.

GARDEN OF STAGHORN CORAL

Vast Coral Fields

Diving down I was immersed in a gaudy variety of marine life. Long fields of multi-coloured staghorn coral stretched out before me, broken every now and then by fan-shaped corals that descended in sculptured stairs. Nearby, a lacey outcrop of tubipora coral hung like a delicately woven Spanish mantilla above a clump of magenta brain coral as intricately detailed as a 19th-Century drawing.

For ten, perhaps fifteen minutes, we glided over, through and under these immense coral fields, absorbed in their unfamiliar beauty and the minute details of the life they supported. There was a pale pink sea anemone with swaying tentacles; close beside it I noticed a striped red clown-fish, watching shoals of smaller fish scurrying by. Then it was time to turn back and make our way to the surface.

SHOAL OF CLUPEID FRY

5/ Spineless Tenants of the Reef

An alien element filled with outlandish shapes so that we feel none of the sympathy, none of the kinships, which often link us to the creatures on land. ARTHUR C. CLARKE/ *THE COAST OF CORAL*

Swimming in the silent waters of the Great Barrier Reef, I had noticed the corals first of all. And then the fish. But as time went on, and my eye became more experienced, I began to discover another fascinating group of creatures that live on the Reef—the many animals without backbones. In the crevices and caverns in among the rocks, sand, mud and sea grasses live unknown numbers of these invertebrates—sponges, anemones, worms, crabs, and all manner of crustaceans, shelled and naked snails, clams, starfish, sea urchins and sea cucumbers—scuttling, slithering, drifting, or rooted to one spot, just waving in the current. One day when I felt I wanted a change from diving down to the coral gardens, I decided to rummage out some of their secrets and perhaps collect a few specimens on the reef flats, where they are best seen and most accessible.

It would be difficult to find a greater contrast on the reefs than that between the underwater coral gardens and these outer reef flats. Here there is no hint of the exotic luxuriance that may lie in deeper water only hundreds of feet away. Stretching before me were the shallows of the flats, broken by the tumbled remnants of blackened reef rock and other debris. To my right was the reverberating surf, pounding on the reef edge. The waves advanced in shimmering, glowering walls. I had to look up to see their crests, and there seemed no reason why they should not rush on and swamp me. But every time the reef edge bore the brunt and I was left miraculously immune, lapped gently by the secondary waves round my shins. Under the harsh monochrome glare of the midday tropical sky, with the incessant drumming of the surf, the flats made a derelict, even mournful scene.

Settling down beside a block of coral that seemed particularly promising, I rolled it back carefully and blundered into an intimate, writhing refuge of creeping crustacea, brittle-stars, worms and small molluscs. A chubby, rounded, smooth crab clung to the surface with great tenacity and around it were soft, creamy growths that could have been sponges. Everywhere were hard little, round, pink blobs firmly attached to the rock. I looked at them closely under a lens and saw that they had a blistery appearance: thinking back to the illustrations in my text-books, I decided that they were encrusting foraminifera, minute animals that hardly seem like living creatures at all. Minute and static, spreading over the dark underworld of rock, they illustrate perfectly how alien is the world of invertebrates to human eyes.

I managed to detach a couple of crabs and dropped them into a jar I had brought with me for the purpose. Suddenly the jar was stirred into a maelstrom with an alarming flurry of legs and pincers. As the storm settled I found that one of my specimens had lost its legs and the other—a paddle-legged swimming crab—was completing a fearsomely efficient dismantling job, prior to eating the first one.

Before leaving, I searched around for some borers and cavity-dwellers. A beautiful white worm, covered in bristles like a caterpillar, was wriggling about, half out of its inner home. I tried to grasp it, and immediately snatched my hand back: I had been stung. It was an unpleasant way to learn about the defences of the nereid worm, and I was glad there was no time left to learn any more lessons. The water had now begun to lap around my knees and was getting rougher as the tide brought the surf closer. I rolled my boulder back into place and headed for the distant shore.

In one short trip I had seen a good deal, but it was only a minute fraction of the invertebrate world. With the extravagance typical of tropical marine life, the invertebrates have diversified into thousands upon thousands of species. So overwhelming is their variety that many are still uncatalogued. To add to the confusion, all these barely known creatures have complex inter-relationships with one another, co-operating, competing, eating and being eaten. Drawing on the sun's energy stored in a rich soup of plant plankton, capitalizing on one another's efforts, they create innumerable food chains, each with many side branches, that build up into complicated food webs. All of which makes these invertebrates impossible to understand at the present time except in the broadest and simplest terms. Further research will, hopefully, clarify some of the perplexities.

Just about the only way so far discovered for disentangling this confusion is to divide up these animals according to their mode of feeding. At the bottom of the food pyramids are the vegetarians, animals whose appetites are satisfied by filtering food particles from the water or by browsing on plants. The creatures one step up are meat eaters and exist by hunting the vegetarians; they in turn are pursued by larger carnivores. Taking advantage of all these activities are various scavengers and parasites.

The simplest vegetarians have the easiest life. They eat tiny, single-celled algae suspended in the plant plankton, which gives them the name of suspension feeders. Since the plankton floats in the water all around them, they have no need to move. All they do is to draw in water, filter out the food particles and then expel it together with any waste products. Since the plankton algae are microscopic, they must collect and digest vast numbers to survive.

Perhaps the most remarkable filters are the sponges, which can process as much as a thousand times their own bulk of water in an hour. The water enters through the hundreds of holes in the sponges' colourful, plant-like bodies, but leaves through a few of the larger openings. This is a special sanitary arrangement to ensure that the waste is discharged well clear of the animal and is not drawn in again. Sponges have no blood system or specialized organs and are little more than aggregations of cells. But these cells are highly adaptable: some of them, for example, possess microscopic whips that line the channels inside the body and, by constant beating, create the flow of water. It is a measure of the success of such adaptations that sponges are found all over the Reef, ranging from lumpy encrustations of bright green, yellow or red on the underside of dead coral to various delicate shapes in deeper water: fans, clusters of fingers, cushions and chalices.

Other suspension feeders are much more elaborately equipped than the sponges. The various bivalved molluscs, like clams, oysters, mussels and cockles, which have a shell consisting of two symmetrical halves or "valves" hinged by a connecting ligament, feed in the same way as sponges. Water enters by one opening, passes through the elaborate latticework of the gills and then leaves through a separate open-

A colony of miniscule, sack-like sea squirts display the frilled openings at the tops of their bodies through which they draw in food-bearing water. After filtering out minute organisms, they expel the strained water through a communal opening hidden in the centre of the colony, spurting it far enough from themselves to avoid polluting the in-coming currents.

ing. Sometimes these apertures are at the ends of long siphons, enabling their owners to live well below the surface of the sea floor and yet draw water from above. Those that do not bury themselves generally secure themselves on the rocky surfaces of the Reef. One kind of clam, *Lithophaga*, actually bores into the coral rock, softening it first, possibly with acid, then scraping it away with its hard shell by heaving itself backwards and forwards on the threads that attach it to the coral. There are exceptions however: the limas or file shells, which have bright red tentacles, swim through the water by flapping the shell-halves rapidly together, and the giant clams—notorious in schoolboy tales for their supposed ability to trap divers in their massive wrinkled "jaws"—stand freely on sand flats or in coral gullies.

The enormous, bulbous shell of the giant clam merges well with its habitat, and it is sometimes disguised with encrustations of coral and other growths. Often it is betrayed only by its soft body, a mantle of green, brown, blue and purple that lines the lips of the shell. Once, as I swam towards a coral cay on the outer barrier, I noticed a giant clam with the two halves of its shell wide open, exposing the luxuriant mantle. It looked so gaudy and so devoid of menace that I decided to dive down and check its legendary reputation for myself.

The clam ignored me as I approached, unlike smaller versions that snap shut when disturbed. I touched the outside of its shell and its purple lips convulsed and rippled in a long shudder, but it showed no signs of closing. Finally I touched the mantle itself with my hand. Immediately the two huge shells began to close on to each other in a series of awkward jerks, like a door on stiff hinges: its movements were slow, and it failed to close completely. But there seemed such enormous force behind those jaws, and so little chance of reversing their movement, that I could see why divers are wary of them. Yet there could be no malice in a clam: its evil reputation is based largely on the mouth-like appearance of its shells, and its camouflage is merely the natural consequence of the passive, still life of a filter-feeder.

Somewhat less passive plankton-catchers dispense with pumps and filters, and trap food particles in a net. The feather-stars, graceful relatives of the starfish, extend their arms like the fronds of a luxuriant fern and interleave them to form a collecting bowl for the continuous rain of algae and debris that streams with the current. The arms and side branches bear tiny sticky "tentacles" known as tube feet, which form a fine mesh. When food comes into contact with these, it is bundled in mucus, passed into grooves on the upper surface of the arms and thence along a conveyor belt of active hairs to the mouth in the base of the body. Feather-stars are not permanently attached to one spot. They move on to new pastures in characteristically idle fashion, by simply casting off and letting the current carry them through the waters, contributing an occasional, graceful wave of an arm for orientation.

Unlike the suspension feeders, which wait for their food to come to them, the second type of vegetarian invertebrates, the plant-eaters, must be mobile. Not that they roam far: because the various algae on which they feed are found everywhere on the Reef, they do not need to. Instead they concentrate on eating, and have developed ingenious adaptations that best utilize Barrier Reef plant life. They feed not only on ordinary seaweeds but also on less familiar ocean plants: hard encrustations on rocks, lime-secreting red or green plants with coral-like branches, and even filaments that penetrate the substance of dead coral. The seaweeds are soft and easy to feed upon, but the others demand quite elaborate adaptations of what pass for jaws, tongue and "teeth", so that they can be scraped or bitten off.

The ideal machine for scraping belongs to the creeping snails and the sedentary coat-of-mail shells (chitons). This device is the radula, a ribbon-like tongue covered with minute teeth, which acts like a flexible file when drawn to and fro. To feed on the algae encrusting a boulder, the snail pushes this out, scrapes it over the rock surface and carries particles back into its mouth. Nerites, periwinkles, topshells and clusterwinks are the most noticeable of these scraping molluscs. At high tide they can be seen in great numbers on the beach rocks between high and low water marks, creeping like marine lawnmowers through the abundant soft growth.

In among these grazing molluscs live their almost sedentary relatives, the limpets and the chitons. They possess especially hard radulas, some with teeth made of iron oxide and silica. These cutters enable limpets and chitons to eat any plant, even the hardest of encrusting algae, and consequently they do not have to roam in search of food. At their most adventurous, they make a short, ponderous patrol at high water. Then before low tide they return to their "homes"—deep, almost circular grooves, created over time with the help of the mollusc's foot. This massive, rounded sucker pulls down with such force that, day by day, the edges of the shell gradually wear away the rock and form a moisture-tight seal protecting the creature against dehydration by the sun.

Perhaps the most adaptable plant-eaters are the urchins. These spine-covered, beautifully coloured creatures occur all over the Reef area, wandering over the coral, wedged in crevices, bristling from the bottom of rocky hollows, burrowing in the sand. They are biters rather than scrapers and have jaws like the powered grab of a crane protruding through the mouth opening on the underside of the hard shell, known as the "test". The five chisel-like teeth are supported by a unique structure of 40 skeletal pieces, analogous to the wires and hinges of the crane's grab and known as Aristotle's lantern after its ancient Greek discoverer. With this powerful mechanism, the urchin can take mouthfuls of rocky encrustations and even chip into the rock itself. Some species also grind with the jaws or the edges of their tests, making burrows in the rock or dead coral where they can possibly dig out embedded plant filaments and certainly collect plant debris that is carried into their shelter.

At least part of the explanation for the sea urchins' success is that they are well defended. As they crunch their way through rocky encrustations or dig out algal filaments, they keep predators at bay with their spines. The slate-pencil sea-urchin, for example, which feeds in crevices and hollows, has finger-like, blunt spines that can measure up to half an inch in diameter and five inches in length. It swivels these to form a structure of girders that jam its body against the walls of its hole and make it impossible to remove without breaking away solid coral. Diadema, on the other hand, the hatpin urchin, is protected by a forest of thin, poisonous and fragile spears that pivot at their bases to menace any intruder (and incidentally protect three species of tiny fish that shelter among them). The variety of such defences makes urchins look very different from one another. Only in death is their underlying shape revealed: the spines drop off, leaving a brittle, globular or heart shaped test covered in intricate, stippled patterns where once the spines were attached.

Other vegetarians are less effectively defended. Slow moving or static, they are protected from the hostile marine world either by shells, which often do not keep predators out, or, in the case of the plant-like sponges, nothing at all. As a result, the next step up the food pyramid consists of a large group of animals that feed on these herbivores. Many of them are molluscs that scrape the fleshy surface of

traps that they are usually well enough supplied with food if they remain still—as they generally do. They are normally found tucked away on sandy patches between corals, their colourful rosettes blooming from the crevices, and can withdraw into their homes if danger threatens from the few fish or browsing sea slugs that are not deterred by their poison. There are many species of anemones—at least 30 or 40 have been discovered in the Capricorn Islands alone—and they vary considerably in size. The smallest is the tiny waratah anemone, which is less than an inch across and has pink-red tentacles arranged much like the Australian wildflower after which it is named. The largest is the giant anemone, stoichactis, a writhing carpet of curling yellowish-pink tentacles measuring three feet across.

Somewhat different are the jellyfish. Passive but not anchored, these languidly pulsating predators secure their prey by means of long, trailing tentacles armed with particularly virulent stinging cells. Any animal that blunders into one of these deadly drift-nets is instantly paralysed and drawn upwards and into the mouth. Although they do move by pulsations of the umbrella-like bell, this action confers little mobility on them, and they are largely at the mercy of water movements. Between December and April, when northerly winds darken the Reef waters with swirling silt, concentrations of dangerous jellyfish—including box jellies or sea wasps that can kill a man in less than five minutes—are carried in from the open ocean, and anyone who enters these waters does so at his peril.

The related but structurally very distinct Portuguese man-o'-war, or "bluebottle" as it is locally termed, is supported on the surface by a bluish gas-filled float a few inches long. Underneath trail tentacles that can extend to great depths and have a venom sometimes compared to that of a cobra. By this means it can fish far below the surface, the prey being drawn up and then digested by a clustering mass of mouths that spread over its body.

In contrast to the languid jellyfish and anemones, the active invertebrate predators are mobile and adventurous, if slow by other animal standards. Some smother their victims by sheer bulk; others stalk or wait in ambush, then poison them; still others specialize in techniques of breaking and entering, rendering the defensive shells of many plant feeders useless.

Chief among those that smother their prey is the bailer shell, so known because of its usefulness to Aborigine boatmen before the appearance of tin cans. It has a huge, fleshy foot up to two feet long protruding from its shell, and uses this tissue to envelop other molluscs, such as the snails and smaller shells that are its normal diet, folding it over them in a great, slimy mass. While the bailer holds on in this way, it brings up its elastic mouth, which protrudes from the end of a mobile proboscis, reaches over the victim like a glove and digests it.

The stalking and poisoning method is considerably more subtle, as the hunting practices of cone shells and octopuses make clear. The cones are supreme among shelled predators for their skill and effectiveness. They hunt by scent, using the long, trunk-like siphon wavering from the narrow end of the shell as a "nose". As this trunk draws in water for respiration, a special internal organ "tastes" the incoming water and tells the cone whether or not it is getting closer to a source of food. When the prey is within touching range, the cone brings into action a specially adapted radula. Instead of being a file with many teeth, this radula consists of a small magazine of up to 20 separate teeth—hollow darts, which under a microscope can be seen to be ferociously barbed. There is an associated poison gland. To kill its prey, the cone stabs out with a dart charged with strong venom. The victim dies almost instantly and is swallowed. The diets of cones can be deduced from the various shapes and patterns that make their shells so decorative and have turned them into collectors' items all over the world. The most common cones have flecks and spots, and eat worms. Others have reddish-brown triangular patterns, and eat molluscs; others still have long, thin shells each with a widely-flared aperture, and are fish hunters. The most virulent poison is secreted by the fish-eating cones, such as *Conus geographus*, which have caused serious and on occasion fatal injuries to people handling them.

More versatile than the cones are their cousins the octopuses, oval-bodied creatures with eight sucker-lined tentacles and a horny, parrot-like beak at the centre. Unprotected by a shell, they have two different styles of hunting, one for the daytime and another for the night. By day they lie in ambush in coral crevices, perfectly camouflaged by their ability to change colour in seconds from brown to white to green to red. Their lairs are revealed only by the empty shells of crabs that, with fish and molluscs, are their normal diet. They grab passing prey with their tentacles, pass them to their mouth and give them a poisonous, crushing bite. By night they stalk their prey around the coral, strike with a swift rush and consume them.

While cones and octopuses concentrate on catching mobile food, other active predators devote their attention to the sedentary limpets,

Three species of jellyfish display the tentacles whose poisonous stinging cells paralyse prey that unwittingly bump into them. Though the sea wasp (near right) swims strongly by contracting the muscles in its transparent "umbrella" up to 150 times a minute, most jellyfish—like the Portuguese-man-o'-war (far right, top and bottom) and the stinging jellyfish (far right, centre)—are weak swimmers, floating almost passively with the current, and may be stranded on shore by a retreating tide.

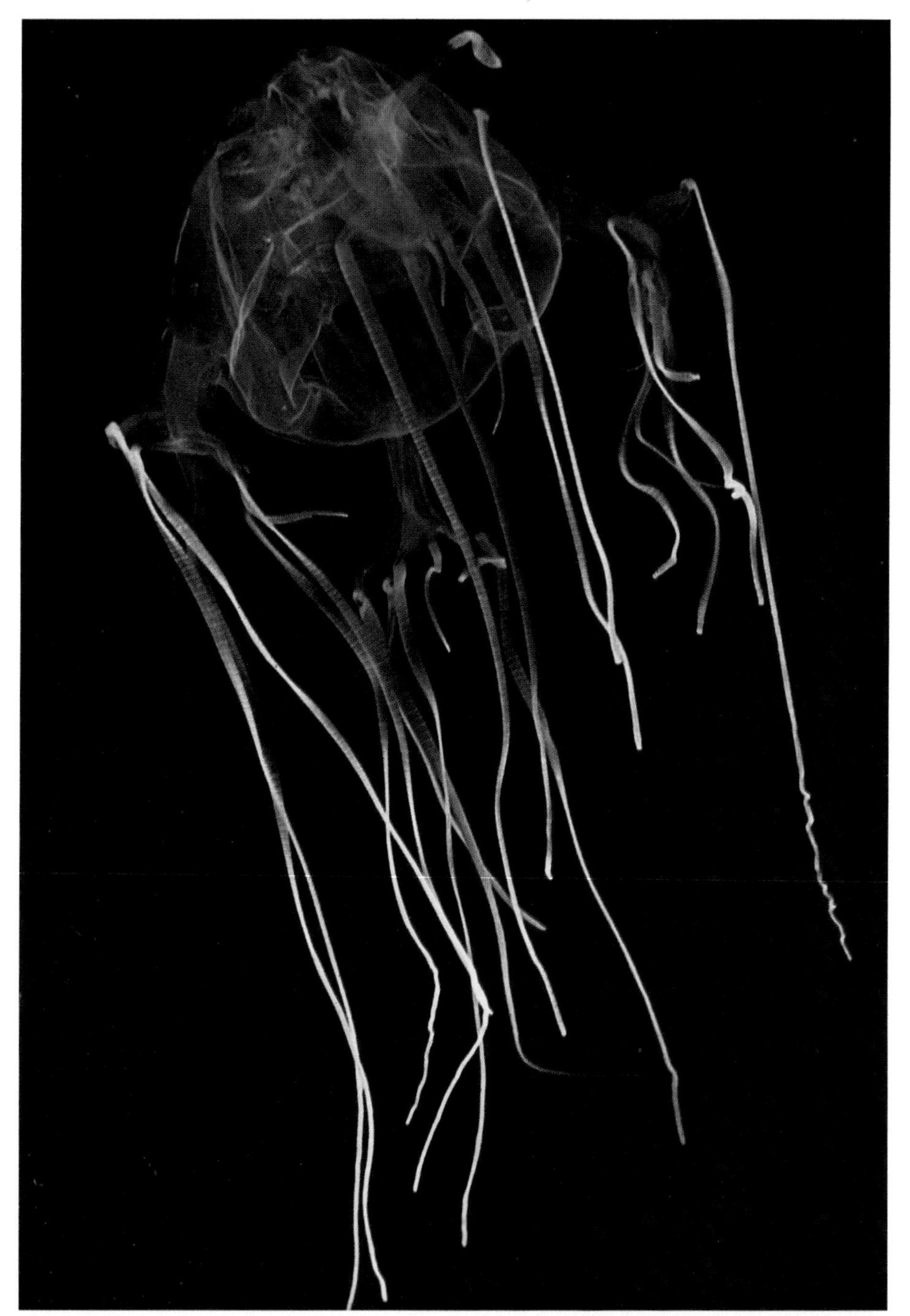

SEA WASP TRAILING ITS TENTACLES

STRANDED PORTUGUESE-MAN-O'-WAR

STINGING JELLYFISH ON SHORE

TENTACLES OF THE PORTUGUESE-MAN-O'-WAR

oysters and bivalves that rely entirely on their shells for protection as they sit, patiently scraping plants or filtering plankton. Any predator that can penetrate the body, either by boring through the shell or forcing it open, gets a meal. In the internecine kingdom of the invertebrates, it would be too much to expect that such an opportunity would be missed, and there is indeed a highly skilled "burglar" class, consisting of certain molluscs and starfish, that spends its time breaking and entering.

The starfish forces an entrance by muscle power. It usually has five arms, though some species have many more, each with a groove underneath into which extend rows of tubular sucker-tipped feet. To eat a mollusc such as a mussel, it attaches its suckers to the two halves of its shell, and pulls them apart with its arms. It can exert a force of up to ten pounds, and as soon as the unfortunate shellfish tires and relaxes enough to open a tiny gap between the shells, the starfish begins the second stage of its meal. It simply turns its stomach inside out through its mouth, inserts it into the gap and begins to digest the occupant. It can even relax while doing so, letting the shells clamp down on its stomach for a while and then forcing them apart again to allow the backlog of digested flesh to run into its body.

The capacity for boring holes is highly developed among certain marine snails, notably the aptly-named drill. It penetrates the shell of the victim, usually a bivalve or an acorn barnacle, by a combination of mechanical and chemical means. The radula is extended at the end of a proboscis, on the underside of which lies an acid-secreting pad. By alternate application first of the acid and then of the scraping radula, a hole is excavated. The drill then inserts its proboscis and brings the radula into action again, scraping away this time at the living animal. Among the other hole-borers, plough shells generally prey on clams, while helmet shells tackle the sea urchins, simply ignoring the spines and going straight into the central shell. In this way, the equally hardy tritons bored and scraped their way into the scientific headlines by preying on the notorious, spiny crown of thorns starfish.

Beautifully patterned, the shell of the textile cone protects a notoriously dangerous animal that crawls along the sea floor poisoning and eating other molluscs and small fish. Its protruding weaponry consists of a fleshy siphon (top right), sensitive to the scent of its prey, and the proboscis (bottom right) housing an arrow-like tooth filled with venom that paralyses its victim.

The invertebrate food pyramids of the Great Barrier Reef, like the immense urban development they resemble, nurture idlers and generate immense volumes of rubbish, providing a variety of extra job opportunities. These are filled by parasites and rubbish collectors.

The parasites are found at all feeding levels, exploiting the food-gathering work of their hosts. Some steal the food and digest it themselves; some let their hosts break it down for them first and then take it away from their intestines; some live on their host's flesh. Those that digest their food for themselves, such as some small shrimps and pea crabs, exploit the possibilities of life within clams and oysters and other bivalve filter feeders. Once drawn into one of them by its food-intake siphon, a shrimp will never have to look for food again. Inside, it will find a constantly replenished supply of finely-divided plant matter covering the net-like gills over which such molluscs constantly strain water. The shrimps are in no danger of joining the rest of the filter-feeder's meal on its path to the stomach: they are far too big to be drawn into its mouth. Consequently, these small crustaceans are unwelcome, but far from lethal guests in nearly every clam and oyster on the Reef.

Far more detrimental to the host animals' well-being are the parasites that live internally, having their food digested for them. The largest are flukes and tapeworms, simple, flat creatures little more than living blotting paper, with complicated life histories. They are passed through a variety of hosts, live on their blood, tissues and digested food and sap their strength.

The more aggressive parasites go after the flesh of their hosts and thrive especially on the ill-fated sea cucumbers. The tiny, spiral *Eulima* snail lives on the outside of the cucumber, piercing its skin with a sharp proboscis and sucking out its body tissues. Small, transparent fish take the process a stage further still by making their homes in the cucumber's anus—living off its reproductive organs. However, this relationship is not as damaging as it might seem: the cucumber is capable of replacing much of its lost tissue and not all these fish are parasitic. Some merely use the cucumber as a base, leaving it at night to feed on a diet of small shrimps, and returning by day.

Far more beneficial to the life of the Reef are the invertebrates that clear up rubbish—dead plants and animals, wasted food, faeces and bacteria. They fall into two major groups, the scavengers, which are content to take soft, easy meals among dead and decaying animals and plants, and deposit feeders, which hoover up vast quantities of sand and mud from which they digest out even the minutest particles of nutritional value. Some scavengers are obvious to any visitor to the Reef, where any rotten flesh left on the sand of a reef flat—perhaps the remains of a large predator's meal—will soon be surrounded by the spiral shells of dog whelks. These snails have a keen sense of "smell" and are usually the first to arrive and start rasping with their minute radulas. Later, the slower, porcelain-like olive shells arrive to feed in the same manner, and any crabs in the area sidle up to grasp and tear with their pincers.

Perhaps the most dedicated scavengers are the hermit crabs, which roam the beaches by night, picking with their pincers for anything edible along the tide line. Even their shells are second-hand, taken over from suitably sized molluscs when the original inhabitants have died. On one reef walk, as I was climbing (with the help of a long reef pole) from the sea bed on to the coral platform, I noticed a small pink shell balanced on an outcrop of coral next to a black bêche-de-mer. I picked it up. The shellfish that used to live within had long since gone, but inside was a tiny multi-hued hermit. This shell was only about two inches long, and the crab itself must have been little more than an inch across; but it sat there, pincers at the ready and long stick-like eyes watching, for all the world like one of the larger and more fearsome rock crabs I had noticed scuttling across the beachrock a few days earlier.

When in search of a home, each hermit crab backs its soft body into whatever shell it chooses so that only its tough head and front limbs are protruding. If it is attacked it will withdraw almost completely within the shell. The crab carries its adopted home upon its back wherever it goes, until it begins to outgrow it: whereupon it has to search around for a replacement. This is a painstaking process, and a crab may inspect and discard several shells before deciding to transfer from one to another. At such moments of decision it is very vulnerable to attack. Often it draws up its old shell close in front of its new home and then quickly scuttles from one to the other. If necessary a hermit crab will actually tear a live mollusc from its shell in order to claim a new home.

Strangest of all the scavengers is the tiny gall crab. I found one during a dive on Wistari Reef. Inspecting some purple coral, I noticed it seemed to fold over a tiny slit, inside which there was an occasional, irregular movement. This was a female gall crab, which settles among growing coral while still very young, and stays there while the coral arches over and imprisons it in an oven-shaped chamber. As the coral grows the crab manages to stir up water currents by moving slightly, maintaining a series of holes through which adequate supplies of edible detritus and plankton move into its cell. The males live a free life outside, but they are small enough to visit the females by climbing through the tiny slit. Eventually, walled up in her coral chamber, but not before discharging great numbers of larvae, the female dies.

At the end of the line are the deposit feeders, which live off the bacteria and minute particles of organic matter deposited on the sea floor and too small to be consumed by the scavengers. These deposit feeders swallow huge amounts of sand and mud, digesting the organic matter to be found in it, and discharging the remainder through the anus. By far the most important animals feeding by this method are the parasite-ridden sea cucumbers: most of the sand along the reefs has at one time or another passed through their long, sausage-like bodies. They are related to the starfish and sea urchins and, like them, move with tiny feet arranged along the sides of the body. Here any resemblance to their relatives ends. Their mouths are at the front of the body (instead of underneath) and they vary from six inches to six feet in length.

Many other animals process mud and sand in much the same way: lugworms tunnel through quite deep sand, some bivalves draw in great quantities of bottom debris and the vast numbers of fiddler crabs turn over mud in the tidal and estuary areas among the mangroves. Together, all these scavengers and deposit feeders complete the food cycle, ensuring that every part of the energy that enters the Reef waters through sunlight and plants is utilized. The clean sands, clear water and abundance of creatures in all parts of the Great Barrier Reef testify to the efficiency of this marine economy.

A Slow-Motion Wilderness

The shallow, warm waters behind the outer ramparts of the Great Barrier Reef form a sheltered, stable environment for an immense diversity of sluggish creatures. There is such a wealth of microscopic food that suitably adapted animals, such as the myriad sponges, can sit and filter an ample diet from these waters without ever moving. These most lazy of reef creatures and the barely more energetic crawlers and drifters, such as sea urchins (opposite) and feather-stars, fill every nook of the coral-strewn sea bed.

When creatures of this sort do move, usually in search of new pastures, their actions are leisurely. Urchins like mobile pin-cushions shuffle on tiny, concealed feet; sea cucumbers ripple ponderously through weeds and over sand. Plant-like anemones either slide, clumsily upright, or somersault by a most laborious process. Holding on with the sucker at the base of the trunk, they reach over and grip with their tentacles, then release the sucker and swing themselves over. Feather-stars looking like palm fronds cast off and drift in the current.

None of these movements is fast enough for the reef creatures to escape their predators, and so they use other methods of defence. Anemones fend off their enemies, mostly sea slugs, with batteries of minute stinging whips. The sea slugs in turn deter other predators, such as starfish, by a variety of ingenious adaptations. The more gaudy of them actually eat the anemones' poisonous cells and use them to their own advantage. These slugs have slimy digestive systems that immunize them against the poison. The cells pass harmlessly through their bodies until they concentrate in tentacle-like growths on the body surface where they function as poison armouries. More dowdy slugs camouflage themselves by feeding only on plants of their own hue.

Urchins are protected by sharp or blunt spines that either prick or poison an enemy or alternatively jam the urchin in a coral crevice so that it cannot be dislodged. Their cousins, the sea cucumbers, are so leathery and slimy that they are equally difficult to get hold of. Some cucumbers are also poisonous, and others ensnare attackers in squirts of sticky threads. Strangest of all, a few species jettison some of their internal organs to keep the enemy occupied, crawl away and grow a new set.

A waving mass of broad, blunt spines protects the brittle shell of a slate-pencil sea urchin. Although less formidable than the sharp needles of other urchins, they are an effective defence against its chief enemy, the starfish. The body is typical of urchins: a rounded case of five chalky plates arranged like the petals of a folded flower. The light-sensitive plates or "eyes" face upwards; the mouth is below, surrounded by tiny "feet".

The petals of the inch-long sea slug Cyrce nigra present a large surface to the water, assisting oxygen intake.

The bright colours of a sea slug warn predators of poison concentrated in the tips of the "fingers" on its back.

The sea hare, Aplysia parvula—named by the Roman writer Pliny who compared them to crouching hares—browses on seaweed, "ears" erect.

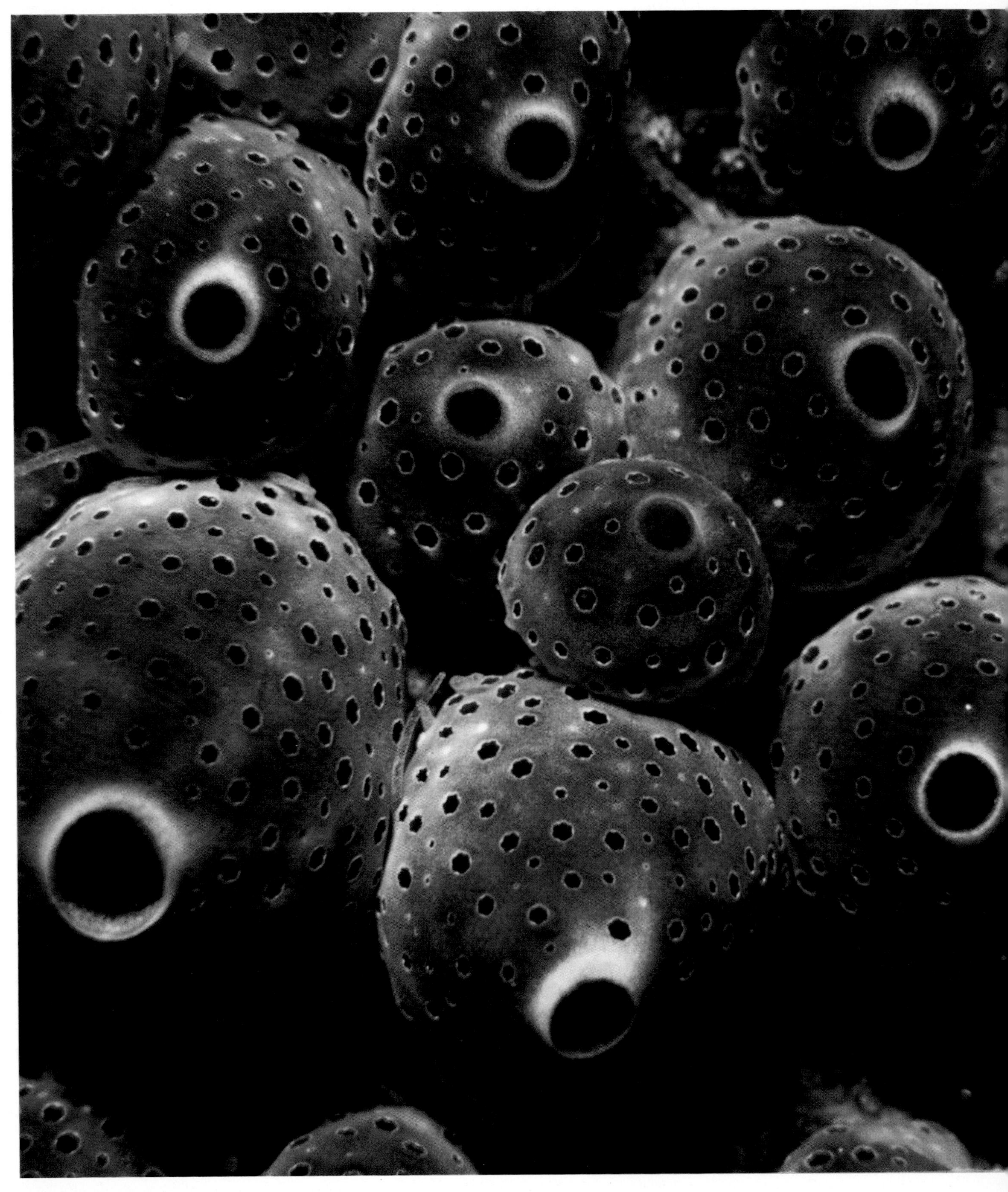

The vase-like, sycon-type olynthus sponges (left) are basically hollow filtration units. They suck in debris-laden water through small holes by agitating microscopic, whip-like hairs inside, digest any organic morsels and eject the rest through the large hole at the top.

A mature sponge flaps passively in shallow-water currents. Although it looks like a plant and is fixed to one spot, it is in fact a simple animal. It has no nerves and little skeleton, and its structure is so elementary that any fragment can grow into a new sponge.

The tiny anemone Calliactis polypus extends its tentacles, their stinging cells ready to repulse intruders or paralyse tiny fish for food.

Presented with a morsel of debris too large for one delicate arm, a rosy feather-star activates all ten limbs to guide it mouthwards.

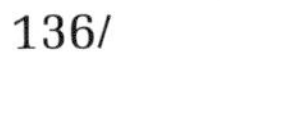

The night feather-star Lampometra palmata spreads its arms wide for food. Particles from the continuous rain of organic debris in the reef waters are trapped on the delicate fronds, bound up in a sticky bundle of slime and passed to the central mouth by thousands of microscopic tentacles.

The sea cucumber Stichopus variegatus (right) ripples across a shallow coral pool in search of a suitable sand patch. It feeds by shovelling sand into its mouth with tentacles and digesting out any plants or animals. As many as 2,000 cucumbers live in one acre of reef, processing up to 60 tons of sand a year.

6/ Haven for Seabirds

Countless . . . birds rose shrieking on every side so that the clamour was absolutely deafening, like the roar of some great cataract. J. B. JUKES/ *VOYAGE OF* H.M.S. "*FLY*"

The Queensland mainland began to disappear in the haze astern, and our 60-foot fishing launch headed out towards the Pacific horizon, a curving knife-edge where the faded, light blue sky met the stronger hue of the ocean. The ship's skipper, Perry Harvey, was taking me to Beaver Cay, one of the innumerable sand cays of the Great Barrier Reef, a tiny stretch of low-lying land without vegetation and inhabited only by a colony of terns. These are the most ubiquitous seabirds of the reef region and we hoped to see them in their own environment.

A manta ray veered away from the bow of the boat. Then a long tom, a thin fish shaped like an oversized garfish, went skipping rapidly across the surface of the water, standing almost upright on a tail that was shaking so fast it seemed to be spinning and propelling the fish along like an outboard motor. Hours later, I noticed birds wheeling in the sky. Beneath them a small sandhill poked up from the sea. It was like a thick pancake, raised a little at one end, and as we drew closer I could make out the remains of a small boat, wrecked to the weather side of the cay. Otherwise the island showed no trace of man.

The surrounding reef stops boats getting close in; so, donning wet suit and snorkel gear, I jumped overboard and set out to swim ashore—though not before Perry Harvey had dragged a bloody fish through the water to make sure that a huge groper that lives off the edge of the cay was not around (and hungry). I swam in over branching acropora coral, giant clams and sea anemones, and at last emerged in the shallow water next to the sandbar. I had arrived on one of the typical seabird colonies of the reef.

As I rested for a moment in the shallows, I reflected on the island's inaccessibility. It had taken several long hours in a fast boat and then a swim to reach it. No other animals, certainly not man, could live here. There is no water on the island, no food source other than the birds and fish, no easy way of bringing in supplies and no chance of making a living. This is true of many islands of the Reef and consequently they remain very much the undisputed kingdom of the birds.

Apart from a few landbirds, most of which use the forested islands as resting places after a long migration and only occasionally live on them, the incumbents are seabirds. For them the isolated conditions are perfect, particularly during the vulnerable time of nesting. On the ground many are clumsy, sometimes ridiculously so: on the mainland they make easy prey for prowling dogs, and their eggs and young are destroyed by grubbing pigs. But here they are threatened by none of these dangers and can breed in peace. In addition they are perfectly placed to reach their food supply, the great shoals of fish, squid and other animals in the upper layers of the reef and ocean waters.

As a result, some of the largest seabird colonies in the world are found on the Great Barrier Reef. Silver gulls and several different species of tern are permanent residents in the region, while other birds, such as wedge-tailed shearwaters, gannets, frigate birds and still more terns spend much of the year ranging widely over the ocean and come to the Reef only to nest and raise their young.

On Beaver Cay, hundreds of the ubiquitous terns manage to find breeding space, despite the fact that the island is no bigger than a large backyard. Terns are close relatives of the gulls, but smaller, more compact and more direct of flight. Rather than glide and drift with the air currents, they move with a steady, determined wing-beat. As I walked out of the water on to the cay, a large flock of them, nesting along the highest part of the sandbank where it fell abruptly into the sea, took off and went wheeling away with harsh cawing sounds. They swooped around in a great circle and most settled straight back on their nests again, no longer uttering their loud cries but instead giving high-pitched, squeaky, echoing calls as they warned each other I was still there. These were black-capped terns, beautifully streamlined when in flight, and seemingly pure white with startling black crests; it was only when they settled down that I noticed some quite large patches of light grey on their bodies.

Since some of the nests were still uncovered while the parent birds circled overhead, I was able to see several eggs. They had been laid straight on to the gritty sand, a coarse bed of coral particles and shell rubble. There were two small, oval, mottled eggs in each nest, well camouflaged against this background. Some were beginning to hatch, and I watched for a while as one dark-speckled egg broke apart and the tiny chick inside began to struggle free. Then I came across some babies that were fully hatched and were squatting on the hot sand, legs tucked underneath them, beaks agape, so sand-coloured and speckled that they merged with their surroundings. In each case there was an unhatched egg beside them.

The parent birds were circling a few yards away and Perry Harvey had warned that if they left the nests for too long their eggs "would fry in the sun"; I certainly did not want to disturb them unnecessarily and moved away towards the northern end of the cay.

Walking down a shell-littered spit of sand, I sat down in the shallows at the end to cool off. It was not long after midday; the sun blazed from an almost colourless sky, and the wind seemed to have dropped. To my surprise, I found myself looking out over the vortex formed by two currents of water: the cay was at the exact point where wind-blown waters washing in from the Pacific Ocean were met by the tide flowing out from the mainland. Where the currents met, a rooster-tail of water spurted into the air. As I sat there, washed alternately by the Pacific Ocean and the coastal tide, I was impressed by the terns' apt choice of a home. Where the water wells upwards and brings debris and plankton to the surface, millions of tiny fish and squid assemble to feed—at a level that is ideal for the terns' specialized hunting methods.

When seabirds hunt, they search and strike in a number of surprisingly different ways. Just as landbirds feed in different layers, from the ground to the tops of trees, so the seabirds exploit different layers in the air and ocean. Each species has its own preferred method and altitude for searching, and its own style and depth of diving. Many of the terns, for example, fly at a moderate height, around 20 to 80 feet, and plunge down to not more than a fathom. The greatest heights are the preserve of the gannets and boobies, goose-sized, powerful birds with straight, sharp bills and wedge-shaped tails. They also dive to the greatest depths. One gannet that followed its prey into a fish trap and was discovered there, drowned, accidentally demonstrated that they go 80 feet below the sea surface and possibly deeper. Flying with strong, slim wings, the gannets possess great strength and stamina, often searching well out of sight of land. When they sight the dark patch in the water that identifies a shoal, they descend to about 100 feet, fold their wings and simply drop. They hit the surface with a tremendous splash at speeds approaching 100 m.p.h., shielded from the impact by air sacs under their skin and exceptionally thick skulls. Once submerged, they "fly" under water to pursue a fish or a squid, catching and swallowing it before bobbing back up, resting briefly on the waves, then flapping strongly back to sufficient altitude for the next dive.

A number of other birds fish quite effectively with a great deal less effort, either sitting on the water and merely dipping in their beaks or skimming food from the surface without even getting wet. Chief among the sitters are the gulls, which are considerably lazier in all their hunting habits than the gannets and most of the terns. Their method of searching is to drift on air currents, slipping and gliding with casual mastery. Like vultures, their land-based counterparts, they search separately—but just in sight of one another. When one bird discovers a shoal of fish or a drift of debris, it gives a cry as it drops and so alerts others nearby. In a surprisingly short time a raucous column of gulls forms, serving as a beacon to every bird for miles around, and the water is covered with bobbing birds busy dunking their heads for food. Gulls can reach as far below the surface as their necks stretch. The nearest attempt they make at a dive is a ridiculous immersion that covers only about half the body—such is their natural buoyancy that they immediately shoot back up like inflated rubber toys.

Several types of bird use the skimming method of hunting, including the white-capped noddy tern, a streamlined and delicate hunter, measuring about a foot from its sharp bill to the tips of its deeply-forked tail. It is among the most agile of seabirds. Scarcely if ever needing to enter the water, it skims the surface with its beak, skilfully snatching food with hardly a missed beat of the wings. The most formidable of this type of fisher is the frigate bird, master of the air and the enemy of all medium-sized birds. With wings that measure as much as seven feet from tip to tip—the largest wing area relative to body weight of any bird—it is supremely manoeuvrable. As a result, it is a virtuoso performer of different hunting styles.

For some 17 weeks after hatching on a Reef island, the masked booby chick is fed whole fish swallowed by the parents at sea and brought back to be regurgitated. When the down-covered chick begs (1), it is allowed to probe in its parent's throat (2). As the food is regurgitated, the chick may topple over (3) but, disengaging itself, it swallows the fish in one gulp (4), comes back and begs for more (5).

1/ CHICK BEGGING FOR FOOD

2/ PROBING FOR FISH

3/ TRANSFER OF FOOD

4/ FISH BEING SWALLOWED

5/ A PLEA FOR MORE

It can skim the waves, snatching fish, squid and young turtles from the surface with its long, hook-tipped bill, disturbing hardly a drop of water (which is just as well, since its feathers are easily waterlogged). So accurate is its aim that it can take a strip of fish from a rock at full speed, without hesitation or accident. Its most spectacular aerobatics are displayed when it turns to aerial robbery. A feeding crowd of seabirds is seldom without its escort of these buccaneers, ready to chase and harry any bird carrying food. Out-manoeuvred, pecked, sometimes even flipped into a spin by a skilful flick of its tormentor's wing, the victim escapes only by dropping its load, giving the frigate bird its chance to swoop on its booty before it touches water.

At the peak of a feeding session around a large shoal, the different feeding techniques can be seen clearly. Hundreds of gulls and the odd brown noddy plunge and bob at the surface, sometimes taking off with choice morsels to be mobbed and screamed at by their companions or harried by the ever-present frigate birds. Terns rocket through the crowd, disappearing occasionally in sudden plunges, while the white-capped noddies steer a skilful path through the confusion, skimming the surface for fragments and small fish.

With the twin conditions of food and safety so fully satisfied on the isolated reef islands, it is not surprising that many seabirds stop during their ocean travels to breed here. The most famous of the long-distance wanderers are the wedge-tailed shearwaters, also known as mutton birds because of their place in Australian culinary history. They can be found as far afield as the Pescadores Islands in the Formosa Straits and the Seychelles Islands in the Indian Ocean. Their ability to fly great distances is legendary.

When the nesting season begins in early summer, all these species, migrants and residents alike, settle down on every patch of land that is suitably placed for their particular hunting styles, congregating in mixed colonies, often several species to a single island. On the cays, such as the one I visited, Beaver Cay, assemble the roaming birds of the ocean regions; the more sedentary types distribute themselves over both cays and continental islands. Some of the colonies are amazingly large and diverse: the 10,000 sooty terns on Raine Island are only one of 13 species to breed there.

On forested cays and continental islands, the trees provide an opportunity for a great diversity of breeding habits. For example, the white-capped noddy terns, smaller and more delicate than most of their relatives, happily opt out of the stiff competition at ground level and build their nests in pisonia trees, using the green-brown dead leaves as building material. The selection of these leaves, often as big as a man's hand, is an elaborate ritual. The male noddy picks one up, and flies with it to his mate who is building the nest. The female bird primps and tests the leaf to see if it is acceptable, and then either adds it to the clumsy pile she is building on the branch, or drops it disdainfully to the ground. The leaves that are accepted are glued together untidily with bird excreta.

The pisonia is the tree whose sticky seed buds can be fatal to the birds that nest in it. I once saw a noddy flapping around helplessly on the ground, one wing glued to its body by a tangle of branches; the rest of its feathers, from beak to tail, were covered in buds each about the size of a jellybean. Unable to fly, it would soon have died. The bird was easy to catch and I began pulling the buds out one by one, gradually untangling the feathers and separating them from each other. The noddy protested at first, and tried to peck at me with its thin beak, but slowly it became more accustomed to the operation and squirmed only when some feathers came away with the deadly buds. The whole process took an hour. Then I set the bird back on the ground, and waited. The noddy got its balance on its webbed feet, shook itself, walked a few experimental paces, and took off on a wavering flight to a nearby tree, where it sat, ruffling its tattered feathers, vexed but apparently unharmed physically.

As well as offering mixed facilities to the noddy terns, trees give the advantage of height to frigate birds. These large creatures are less adaptable than terns and although their aerial finesse is superb, they are appallingly clumsy on land. In particular they find it hard to take off and have to rush, staggering and stumbling, down the steepest slope available. In comparison to this, a tree is a luxury, for it allows them to make a swift downwards acceleration. Consequently, when trees are available, most frigate birds nest in them. Some of these predatory birds, however, forgo the pleasures of easy take-off in favour of squatting on cays where terns and gulls have large colonies. There they can plunder the other birds' eggs and chicks, or follow the flock to find food. Furthermore, the watchful terns around them give advance warning of intruders and allow the frigate bird to get airborne.

On both nesting sites, the frigate birds stage elaborate and flamboyant breeding displays. The males possess an immense, inflatable, scarlet sac on their throats, a sort of bright sexual waistcoat that they press into use as soon as the breeding season begins. Unlike most birds, frigate males are not aggressive towards one another in the breeding season, and they are quite content to put on their sexual display communally. The act begins when several males form a group on the beach and inflate their sacs. Whenever a female passes, they shiver and rattle their feathers to attract her. Tempted by this multiple stimulus, she descends and chooses a mate. If not courting with a group, a male puts a couple of twigs on a branch or a patch of high rock to establish ownership, sits on them to confirm it, and then blows up his scarlet sac to attract a mate and warn off competitors. Once a female has succumbed to the charm of this display, she brings her mate nesting material, such as leaves and dead twigs, frequently snatched on the wing with the skill for which frigate birds are deservedly famous. The male adds them to bones and feathers to form an untidy nest that he then rarely leaves, since it is his task to be the guard. All sea birds are thieves, but frigate birds are masters of the art and the nest is in danger from the moment two twigs are put together. Neighbouring frigate birds filch the building materials, snatch eggs and think nothing of making a meal of unattended young. After 15 days, however, the female relieves the male for a further 15-day spell. This alternation occurs again until the single white egg hatches, after about six weeks.

Space on the Great Barrier Reef islands is so fully exploited by the bird population that even the earth underground is pressed into service. Beneath the trees of many cays there are innumerable burrows built by shearwaters. These dull brown birds, about a foot long with narrow wings and a hook-tipped beak, have sharp claws on their webbed feet and thick, calloused outer toes, and excavate by lying first on one side and then on the other, throwing clouds of sandy dirt into the air behind. In the holes so built, eggs and young are safe from the dangers of surface and tree breeding. Shearwaters start building in the late spring, sometimes timing their arrival on a particular island to exactly the same date as the year before. They immediately begin work on their burrows, which look like rabbit diggings. Although usually less than 18 inches long, the tunnels sometimes stretch to nine feet; on some islands the ground is undermined for hundreds of yards, so that it is impossible to walk without crashing a leg through it.

Shearwaters return to the same nest year after year, and are expert renovators. Even after a cyclone they seem to prefer to dig out their old nests rather than create new ones. Once the burrows have been made habitable, the shearwaters can be seen resting at the entrance, squatting heavily on the ground in much the same attitude they adopt on open water. Then they start courting, raising a barrage of sound as they rub bills and cackle to one another. The pairs follow this with a two to three week "honeymoon flight" out to sea, where they fish and build up food reserves before settling down to the long arduous process of bringing up a family. On return, a single white egg, about the size of a small hen's egg, is laid in a nesting bowl in the end of the burrow. Both parents share the incubation, in alternate shifts of 12 to 14 days, until the chick hatches after about eight weeks. Throughout each long incubation shift, the sitting parent takes no food or water, while the other gorges itself at sea in preparation for its own hungry vigil. The non-sitters take off in the mornings, about five o'clock, to feed and gather food for the chicks. The birds' heavy bodies and narrow wings make take-offs difficult and they need plenty of space; they run over the ground like heavily-laden airliners, wings held aloft, banging into each other, until finally they manage to get airborne and disappear out to sea.

Their return at dusk is a dramatic moment in the daily life of an island. As the evening light dims, a roar of wings heralds the arrival of thousands of shearwaters, which circle and patrol the island uttering no calls, but rushing ever-lower, ever-nearer—probably looking for the familiar contours of their own nest burrows. About three-quarters of an hour after the flock arrives over the island, the first bird comes in, retracting its legs and folding its wings about four feet above the ground, and lands with a heavy thump, its fall unbroken by any spreading of wing or tail feathers. The bird then scoots for its burrow, where it is met by its mate. Shearwaters call to one another with weird, high-pitched wails, and as more birds land, the ghostly crying wells up around the island. It goes on all night, and in the unlit pisonia forest, it can be unnerving. If a bird enters the wrong burrow the yowling reaches a sudden crescendo and it is accompanied by much flapping of wings and disturbance of the colony.

So great are the advantages of the reef environment that some land-birds are found here as well, operating as small groups among the far more numerous seabirds or living in self-contained colonies on certain continental islands. They bring with them the distinctive and more complex ways of life found on land. Unlike seabirds, which all eat fish, squid and shrimps and spend their lives almost constantly roaming in search of food, landbirds are used to a more settled, domestic life, close to localities where most of their needs can be met.

Some fresh-water hunters, accustomed to lakes and riversides, are capable of fishing in salt water as well. Several of them, including some herons, waders and eagles, have no qualms about joining the feast at the Great Barrier Reef. The herons, tall, stilt-legged stalkers of tiny fish in the shallows, are the most easily-noticed, land-based birds found in reef waters. In spite of their timidity, they can often be seen in groups as large as 10 or 20 on the foreshores of Green Island, off Cairns, and on Heron Island itself. At low tide they stalk patiently across the reef flats or poise, absolutely motionless, on an exposed lump of coral until, with a flurry of wings, they dive forward and spear unwary fish with their sharp beaks. Groups of their untidy nests litter the upper branches of trees on some of the islands. I saw herons of two different colours grouped around the nests on Heron Island, making patches of blue-grey or white against the greenery. They are both of the same species, but the blue-grey are predominant in the south and the white nearer the Equator. In spite of the fact that both types mingle along the length of the Reef and interbreed freely, there are never any gradations of colour, but only the white and the blue-grey, a phenomenon similar to the occurrence of blue and brown eyes in human populations.

The white-breasted sea eagle, a powerful predator with a four or five-foot wing span and deeply-hooked bill, has also adapted to salt-water hunting. Intent on larger prey than the waders pursue, it patrols the sea by day, soaring on wide wings, or watches from a high perch in a tree, ready to swoop on any fish swimming in the shallows and snatch it with its talons. It tends to nest on the least accessible islands, such as the cay that Captain Cook's naturalists named Eagle Islet when they discovered a sea eagle nest there in 1770.

Although most landbirds on the Reef take their food from the sea, there are a few that use a reef as a dormitory suburb, setting up house on a safe, isolated island and commuting to the mainland to continue their normal feeding habits there. The Torres Strait pigeons are the most conspicuous of these commuters, flying high up in straggling flocks to the mainland in the mornings and returning low across the waves in the evening, with stomachs full of berries and wild nutmeg. At one count an estimated 48,000 of these pigeons made the crossing during an hour and a half of the late afternoon. Droppings from these birds contain seeds, and help colonize islands with vegetation. Falling on otherwise barren cays, the seeds take root, grow into plants and so provide habitats for new settlers.

A very few landbirds satisfy all their needs on the Great Barrier Reef. Were it not for these additions to the local population, the bird life of the region would be as drab and uniform as any dormitory suburb. There is a distinct monotony, even a harshness about fish-eating birds, with their bleak cawing and mewing, their nomadic homelessness and their careless nests scraped out of shell-grit sand. The landbird that does most to break the spell is the silver-eye, a tiny green bird with a clearly marked circle round the eye. It is one of the Reef's rare songbirds and one of the few to take trouble over building its nest. It finds all its food on the islands, feeding chiefly on wild figs, small red and green fruit not unlike tiny crab-apples. I once tried to track down a silver-eye that was singing in the central forest of a reef island, hoping to catch a glimpse of it and perhaps also have a look at its nest. I did not expect the task to be easy, for the bird is well camouflaged and very shy. On the way inland, I disturbed some noddy terns which set up a frightful racket, drowning the tiny, lonely voice of the silver-eye. By the time the noddies had stopped squawking, it was silent. Nevertheless, I continued towards the point I thought its song had come from, and almost stepped on a silver-eye nest that had been blown to the ground, not far from a wild fig tree. It was small, circular and deep-centred, built meticulously of tree fibres and casuarina needles. Normally it would be suspended from branches with neat stitches, like a tiny hammock. The abandoned nest was the closest I came to the songbird, for it did not reveal itself. Standing there with this tiny, delicate thing, I was reminded again of the impermanence of the seabird's way of life: it takes a landbird like the silver-eye to create this painstaking, deftly woven symbol of permanence and domesticity.

Raucous Masters of Air and Water

At breeding time on the Great Barrier Reef, seabirds can be seen from afar, hanging over it like a swarm of midges in the balmy sunlight of a quiet summer's evening. Close to, the illusion of peace is shattered. Myriad birds, chiefly terns, chatter and scream raucously overhead or swoop down through the commotion and dive-bomb intruders with almost scientific precision. Such aerial skill is typical of the seabirds, which are absolute masters of their environment, supremely adapted for flight.

The power-diving gannets and boobies are among the fastest birds of the Reef; they have sturdy wings set far down a completely streamlined body, giving them an outline reminiscent of a jet aircraft. They even slow down rapidly the way a jet does: they open "air brakes" and "parachutes", spreading wide their tails and thrusting their large webbed feet forward into the airstream. Slightly less fast, but also well adapted for diving, are the tropic birds, conspicuous in flight by their streaming tail-feathers.

The wedge-tailed shearwaters are a complete contrast: lightly built, with long, narrow wings, they are superb gliders. Often banking nearly at right angles to the water's surface, they utilize the slightest breeze and rarely flap their wings.

Masterly fliers as these birds are, there is one species on the Great Barrier Reef that can out-manoeuvre them all: the frigate bird. Though clumsy on land, the frigate bird is a living superlative in the air. It has a wing-span of around seven feet—proportional to its weight, the largest of any bird in the world. It has 25 per cent more flight feathers than most other species of birds and this gives its wings a total surface area 40 per cent greater than the average. To use these vast wings, the frigate bird possesses enormous pectoral muscles, which account for approximately one quarter of its total body weight.

During the greater part of the day, these birds soar effortlessly on air currents, wings motionless, occasionally giving bursts of acceleration in aerobatic manoeuvres for food. They are the most aerial of seabirds—probably only the swift spends more time on the wing. Outside the breeding season, they do not touch land during the day at all. After taking off at dawn, they ride the air currents until sunset, when they return to the Reef to roost.

A flock of sooty or "wideawake" terns approach their nesting area. Such colonies are densely packed and landing requires considerable aerobatic skill. The terns are particularly well equipped for the feat. Also known as "sea swallows," they have—like swallows—long, deeply forked tails that can be spread and used both as air-brake and rudder. This enables them not only to change direction with startling rapidity but also to stop dead in the air before landing.

This masked booby is at its most streamlined, the feet tucked under the tail and the bill extending the contours of the head.

Lesser frigate birds use air currents to soar without flapping their wings.

A sooty tern manoeuvres with its tail spread.

The red-tailed tropic bird approaches the camera, trailing its long tail-feathers—devices for display rather than aids to flight.

Silver gulls—the only small birds of this type found on the Great Barrier Reef—hover above a coral rock before landing. Like most gulls, they have a distinctive method of hovering: they ride on wind that has been deflected over an obstacle, such as a rock or cliff, making constant adjustments to their body shape with movements of their wings and feet. The wings can be swivelled and the feathers spread or closed and the dangling feet can be swung backwards or forwards to alter the centre of gravity and so keep balance.

7/ A Future of Uncertainty

A thousand interacting and balanced forces, like the flying buttresses of a towering Gothic cathedral.

C. M. YONGE/ *A YEAR ON THE GREAT BARRIER REEF*

The Great Barrier Reef is still a wilderness area today because it has been protected by its inaccessibility and by the dangers of navigation. But it may not always remain so: in the face of modern technological development, these natural barriers can no longer guarantee its future. The Reef is now—in the opinion of various would-be developers—a tempting prize ripe for the picking. Already the entire coastland facing the Reef and the Reef itself have been parcelled out in oil exploration and mining permits. Attempts have been made to mine the coral islands for limestone, used as fertiliser in sugar-cane farming. Tourists "fossick" for corals and take home rare shells as souvenirs, and island resorts have sprung up to cope with an influx of trippers who bring problems of water supply and sewage disposal.

All these man-made threats seriously affect the ecological balance of the reef system. Gathered together under the fashionable, but nonetheless valid, title of "marine pollution", they have been blamed for the most notorious and immediate threat facing the Reef—the infestation of the crown of thorns starfish, a voracious creature with such a taste for polyps that it is eating up great stretches of the coral forming the Great Barrier Reef.

The crown of thorns, *Acanthaster planci*, is large for a starfish: on average it measures between 12 and 20 inches across, although 24 inches is not unheard of and the largest specimen recorded so far had a diameter of 28 inches. The crown of thorns also has an exceptionally large number of arms: from nine to 23, with 16 the most common in Australian waters. Most starfish in contrast have only about five arms.

The upper surfaces of the animal are covered with wicked-looking spines from which it derives its name. These are between one and a half and three inches long and are sheathed in a kind of skin that when broken produces a venom. Its effect on human beings varies from a mildly pleasant form of anaesthesia to vomiting and a sharp pain that can last as long as 24 hours.

Along the undersides of the numerous arms of the crown of thorns there are, as in other starfish, an array of tubelike feet equipped with versatile suckers which are its means of locomotion and adhesion to the coral. These act also as sensory organs, enabling the starfish to react to light variations (it prefers the dark, and moves from shadow to shadow). The colour of the starfish adjusts to its habitat. It is generally well camouflaged against the varied hues that are to be found on the living reef: the upperside of its body has mingled spots of grey, red, fawn and green, while the arms are bluish-grey and black and the tips of the spines are reddish-orange.

Even more formidable than the animal's anatomy are its carnivorous feeding habits. It is one of the few creatures to devour coral polyps with noticeable effect. Its method of eating is as simple and efficient as that of other starfish. It crawls on to a piece of coral, everts its stomach through its mouth and brings the stomach lining into direct contact with the coral surface. It then digests the polyps and other tissues and moves on, leaving behind a whitened, dead-coral skeleton.

In this manner a single starfish can feed on an area approximately half its size at any one time. Robert Endean, Reader in Zoology at the University of Queensland, Chairman of the Great Barrier Reef Committee and one of the first marine biologists to be alarmed by the starfish infestation, has estimated that one adult starfish can eat the polyps from about 17 to 23 square inches of branching coral a day, or about seven square feet a week. When there is a plague of many thousands of starfish, this rate of destruction can account for a great deal of coral over a few years.

Scientists do not, in fact, refer to the starfish infestations as a "plague", which implies that their numbers are either undesirable or unnatural, or both. Instead they speak academically of an "aggregation", which is a simple description of the starfish's habit of cramming round the same table to feed. For, as members of the Cambridge Coral

Research Group working in the Red Sea discovered, starfish tend to assemble each night at the same point of feeding, even ignoring other tempting morsels of coral en route. Clearly they are guided by some powerful signal, rather in the same way that gulls searching for food might be alerted by the dive of one bird in the flock. The starfish's signal appears to be some product of its digestive process that drifts away in the water and is detected by other starfish probably through sense organs located in some of their versatile sucker-tipped feet. The result is stupendous. Once the aggregation is in full swing, the crown of thorns degenerate into an invertebrate version of a "feeding frenzy"—a phenomenon common among fish and other animals—and start to feed during the day as well, thus greatly accelerating the rate at which the coral polyps are devoured.

To compound the problem, the crown of thorns starfish breeds very fast in its feeding grounds. At the beginning of the month-long breeding season in December and January, a single female bears between 12 and 24 million eggs, releasing them into the water where they are fertilized by a milky cloud of sperm from the male. This apparent extravagance is not exceptional among starfish, which have to produce in large quantities in order to counteract the vulnerability of eggs and larvae to the numerous planktonic animals that eat them, as well as the very coral polyps preyed upon by the adults. But here is the crux. If there are no polyps left, the eggs and larvae are no longer threatened by one of their chief predators and have more chance to mature into adults. Moreover, the bare skeletons of dead coral provide innumerable safe nooks and crannies where the larvae may settle and grow, half an inch a month, into adolescent starfish. By the time they are two years old and about a foot across, they are able to start breeding themselves. The algae and soft corals that often colonize the dead reef also provide food and protection. In this way the feeding and breeding habits of the crown of thorns starfish interact to fuel the population explosion.

The crown of thorns not only eats and reproduces prodigiously: it also has, in common with other starfish, an extraordinary ability to regenerate, which makes it extremely hard to kill. If any of its arms are cut off, it simply grows new ones. Even if it is chopped up, a whole new starfish (or even several) can usually grow from one or more bits. The only way to prevent it regenerating is to slit it open and gut it of its stomach and gonads.

With all these qualities, crown of thorns starfish can produce

The most notorious enemy of the living reef is the giant crown of thorns starfish, the sinister mass of venomous red, green and brown spines illustrated in these three photographs. Spanning up to 28 inches with as many as 23 arms, it strips the polyps from hard, reef-building coral, leaving only a lifeless limestone skeleton (far right, foreground). It shows a marked preference (top right) for staghorn coral. Sometimes (bottom right) the starfish itself falls victim to the giant triton which traps it and guts it.

CROWN OF THORNS EATING STAGHORN CORAL

GIANT TRITON ON CROWN OF THORNS

WHITE CORAL SKELETON AND CROWN OF THORNS

devastating effects on the Reef. In a single year, for example, they almost completely destroyed the live coral of the fringing reef at Fitzroy Island; Slashers Reef and Lodestone Reef were also heavily attacked and enormous damage done to the first.

All this happened very recently. The first reports about large numbers of these previously quite rare animals began to appear in the early 1960s, when they were observed on several Indian and Pacific Ocean reefs. They have since been found over a wider area, from the Red Sea to Tahiti and on the Great Barrier Reef have increased in numbers at an explosive rate. In 1966, members of a scientific survey of the Reef counted 5,750 of them in a period of 100 minutes on one small area around Green Island, off Cairns. In the following years the starfish went on to devastate most of the surrounding coral. Large areas of the Reef between Cooktown and Townsville have been stripped and the starfish are now moving steadily southwards. Between 1969 and 1971, they moved over 100 miles south from Townsville and in 1972, dense infestations were reported off Bowen and as far south as Line Reef, which is only 26 miles north-east of Hayman Island in the Whitsunday group. It seems only a matter of time before they reach the southern region.

On the question of what caused this population explosion scientists are divided. Comparatively little is known about the creatures: no one had any reason to study them thoroughly before they achieved notoriety. One answer suggested by Dr. Endean is that fishermen and shell collectors have reduced the numbers of the triton shellfish, *Charonia tritonis*, which preys on the adult crown of thorns. The triton is capable of devouring the starfish without any ill effects; later it regurgitates the indigestible spiny parts. However, the triton is not a strikingly effective predator: it has been calculated that it can consume two crown of thorns a week at best. A more general theory, advanced by both marine experts and conservationists, is that man-made pollution has destroyed or altered the conditions that naturally kept the starfish in check. Theo Brown, a marine research associate of the World Life Research Institute of Colton, California, claimed that pollution "resulted in a drastic reduction of predatory pressures during one or more stages of the life cycle of the starfish," and it is surely significant that, unlike many other marine animals, the crown of thorns does not appear to be affected by marine pollution. It may even thrive on it: sea urchins, to which it is closely related, have proliferated near sewage outlets on the United States Pacific coast and many crown of thorns outbreaks have been associated with regions that support considerable concentrations of human population.

Some marine scientists maintain that the infestation could be a cyclical phenomenon, that the Reef may be naturally subject to periodic attacks of the crown of thorns on a large scale. Others reply that there is no evidence to support this theory. But then, only in the last 30 years has equipment been available to carry out proper underwater observations, and perhaps evidence of earlier infestations has simply not come to light. The Cambridge group that observed substantial aggregations in the Red Sea in 1970 found them greatly reduced the following year and almost non-existent by 1972. These scientists investigated several possible predators and concluded that a combination of the trigger and puffer fish had helped to reduce the Red Sea starfish population. But it is doubtful that such predators could stop starfish in a large scale infestation such as that which has occurred on the Great Barrier Reef.

Until the mechanisms of the infestation are known, the vexing question of whether man should interfere cannot be solved. So often when tampering with the delicate mechanism of ecological balance he leaves things worse than he first found them through ignorance of the far-reaching effects he may set in motion. Australia has already received two salutary lessons in the dangers of ecological tampering, the first involving rabbits and the second toads. The story of the rabbits began innocuously enough in 1859 when a dozen pairs of these voracious mammals were introduced from Britain by a settler farmer in Victoria. Six years later the newcomers had multiplied to 10,000, despite the farmer's desperate attempts to control them: he had killed a further 20,000. This alarming trend continued and since five rabbits eat as much as one ewe, the Australian sheep industry was soon suffering. No cure seemed to work and the outlook appeared bleak until in 1950 it was discovered that European rabbits were extremely vulnerable to the virus *Myxomatosis cuniculi.* A few of Australia's unwelcome rabbits were innoculated with this disease, which spread like the Black Death, killing more than 90 per cent of the rabbit population. Soon afterwards, however, there was an alarming development: the survivors became immune to the disease, so making possible a great rabbit revival at some time in the future.

A second lesson was learned the hard way when scientists attempted to control the beetles that damage sugar-cane crops. They latched on to the fact that in South America, where such beetles also live, they were limited by a local predator, *Bufo marinus*, the poisonous giant toad. A consignment of toads was duly imported but, soon after arrival, they abandoned cane beetles for other native Australian insects, and the cane beetle had to be controlled by poisonous insecticides, with side-effects damaging to the long-term ecological balance. Furthermore, the toad, which secretes poison through its skin and puffs itself up in the throats of animals that attack it, has now caused the death of predatory snakes and birds vital to the control of many other pests. Its mating has so packed ponds and water-holes with spawn that the water has become undrinkable.

No such radical attack has yet been made on the crown of thorns in case the cure should be worse than the disease. Instead, two more cautious measures have been experimented with. The first involves "fishing" the predators out of the sea using heavy gloves or a long steel spike, and disposing of them, mostly on land. In the second, the starfish are injected with a poison, such as ammonium hydroxide, which can be assimilated without ill effect in the marine environment. For this a diver uses a huge hypodermic syringe that looks not unlike a bicycle pump tipped with a long needle. Both methods, in requiring extensive time and manpower, are expensive. But in introducing no unknown creatures there is little danger that they could radically upset the ecological balance of the Reef.

Although regions of the Great Barrier are under an immediate threat from the crown of thorns, it is also beset by other, separate dangers, including some familiar blights of advanced industrial environments: mining, oil rigs, tourists and wrecked ships. On March 3, 1970, the *Oceanic Grandeur*, a tanker with a cargo of 55,000 tons of crude oil, ran aground on an uncharted reef in the Torres Strait. Holes 200 feet long were ripped in its side and oil began to spill into the sea. The tanker was on its way from Sumatra to Brisbane and could have taken a longer, safer route. Instead, like many other tankers, it attempted to take a short-cut through one of the riskiest passages in the world—and failed. Its grounding was hardly surprising: three years earlier the Great Barrier Reef Committee, which is comprised of scientists and others concerned about the future of the Reef, had warned that the route was unsafe for vessels with a draught of 38 feet or more. Their warnings, however, were ignored by the state government of Queensland and by the shipping companies: the draught of the ill-fated *Oceanic Grandeur* was exactly 38 feet.

Luckily another tanker carrying ballast was in the area and most

A colony of lobophyllia coral lies shattered on the sea bed in the wake of a cyclone. Lobophyllia is especially brittle because its green polyps create spear-like skeletons anchored only to a central stem. But all corals are vulnerable to natural destructive forces and their self-repairing ability, proved over tens of thousands of years, offers some hope of their capacity to survive contemporary threats as well.

of the stricken ship's cargo was transferred to it. A combination of calm seas and windless days stopped the slick from reaching parts of the Reef where it could have caused irreparable damage. Detergents, which are themselves a pollutant, were used to disperse the oil and the *Oceanic Grandeur* was taken off for dry-docking in Singapore. Conservationists breathed a sigh of relief, but it had been a narrow escape.

Although damage by shipping can be made less likely by legislation, it is harder to stop mining, where vast sums of money are at stake. Recent years have seen an extraordinary minerals boom in Australia, and huge resources of iron ore, bauxite, oil, gas and other natural riches have been discovered. Without the knowledge of most Australians, the Queensland government granted permits to oil companies to drill on the Reef itself. (In 1973 the Premier of Queensland, J. Bjelke-Peterson, was a major shareholder in an oil exploration company that had applications for prime leases in the area of the Torres Strait.) Drilling started on the Reef in the late 1960s. One exploratory bore was sunk on Wreck Island, in the southern part of the Reef, and another in 1969 in the far north-east. Both were unsuccessful, but the oil companies' interest did not abate and by 1970, drilling permits had been given for about 80 per cent of the Reef, an area of approximately 80,000 square miles. Some conservation organizations seemed to accept the mineral exploitation of the Reef as inevitable. In a report on "controlled exploitation" the Great Barrier Reef Committee wrote: "Exploitation of the mineral resources of the area has scarcely begun but exploitation on a large scale is imminent." Not all conservationists took the same amenable attitude as the committee. They believed that any sort of drilling for oil in the Reef region carried with it the risk of an oil blow-out or spill such as the disastrous one at Santa Barbara, off the Californian coast, that caused irrevocable damage to the marine environment there. The Great Barrier Reef is even more vulnerable: it is an enclosed water system that would tend to preserve any oil spillage. Moreover, since cyclones hit the region every two or three years, oil operations would be even more hazardous than in most other places.

The level of exploitation and its attendant dangers were not dramatised for the public until 1970, when an oil rig was about to start drilling in Repulse Bay, a few miles from the tourist resorts of the Whitsunday Passage. Suddenly, Australians were alerted, and a campaign to "Save the Barrier Reef" was launched. A major battle ensued: conservationists versus oil companies, the Australian Commonwealth (or central) government versus the Queensland state government, the public right versus the private interest. The Commonwealth government, led by the then Prime Minister, John Gorton, came down on the side of those who wished to protect the Reef, and prepared legislation to give the Commonwealth government control of the continent's off-shore waters, taking over the powers which had formerly been held by states such as Queensland. The Queensland government, led by Bjelke-Peterson, maintained there was no danger and resisted the Commonwealth's "interference".

In the outcry that followed, the Repulse Bay drilling was postponed and a wide-ranging Royal Commission was set up to inquire into oil exploration on the Barrier Reef and its possible dangers. In 1972, the Labour Party came to power, having pledged itself to take over all off-shore waters (and oil rights), and, so it said, to protect the Barrier Reef.

Even if the Reef escapes the threat of oil exploitation, its other minerals are a lure for industrialists and developers. The most obvious of these is limestone, of which the reefs consist: it could be used as agricultural fertilizer or in the production of cement. The first attempt to mine the Reef was made by the sugar farmers of the Cairns district in the late 1960s. Their application to mine Ellison Reef off Innisfail, south of Cairns, was turned down, however, after marine experts testified about the damage that mining operations could do to the Reef. Even so the Queensland government, in refusing the permit, stubbornly added that "the decision does not mean that the position cannot be reviewed at some future time".

Among the other dangers facing the Reef is tourism. Every year scores of thousands of people visit the more accessible islands and cays: holidaymakers, fishermen, skin-divers, boat-owners, water-skiers and just plain sightseers. Most of them are Australians, though some come from overseas, especially Americans. Tourist hotels have been constructed to accommodate the influx, and underwater observatories—commercial aquaria of reef-life deftly packaged for the tourist's pleasure—have been built on Hook and Green Islands.

As more and more people pour in every year, so the pressures on the Reef increase. Shell collecting, for instance, is a hobby all over the world, and the Reef has been a rich source of shells. But since molluscs are comparatively localized creatures and sometimes are found only on a single reef, certain varieties are in danger of disappearing. The Queensland government has now banned shell collecting except within certain specific limits—though numbers of illegal shells still reach the souvenir market. Spear fishing, too, is a threat; though banned in some waters, it is still permitted elsewhere and many Great Barrier Reef fish are easy targets for skin-divers.

To allow people to see the Reef without harming it conservationists have suggested that tourism be limited to established tourist centres, and that the rest of the Reef should become a series of national parks, reserves, marine sanctuaries and limited access regions. A complete ban upon shell and coral collecting and spearfishing has also been proposed. Some co-ordinated plan for protecting the Reef from its own popularity needs to be worked out in the near future.

A more complex threat is posed by the development of the Queensland mainland facing the Reef. As industry, agriculture, mining and other development have increased, so has pollution. Sewage is pumped into the open sea from the towns along the coast; harbours are dredged, land reclaimed and factories built. Some offshore reefs have already been silted over, and the immense amount of insecticides, pesticides and fertilizers that run into the sea from the farms (especially sugar-cane farms) are a serious hazard. A popular pesticide among the cane farmers is D.D.T. which is valued because of its low cost and its failure to decompose easily and disappear—the very quality that makes it a serious factor in offshore pollution. D.D.T. is absorbed by small fish and passed from one predator to another in increasingly powerful concentrations until some creatures high up in the food chain, such as birds, weaken or fail to breed.

It is hard to imagine what areas of the Reef would be like say 30 years from now if the present threats to its ecology continued unabated. I got some idea when I swam over one area east of Tully, where the Reef has been attacked and left bare by its most immediate enemy, the hungry crown of thorns starfish.

The devastation was even worse than I had expected. Some isolated patches of brilliant coral remained. The rest looked like a wasteland. Forests of weird, dead staghorn coral stretched everywhere. Often the tips of the coral were a glowing luminous purple, but beneath was a rotted mass, like waterlogged swamp wood, covered in slime and a dirty brown algae. All around me, as far as I could see, what used to be a living coral reef stretched dead and lifeless.

At other times and other places on the Reef, this macabre scene seems as remote from reality as the Apocalypse—yet even so one receives the occasional sharp reminder of man's power to interfere with nature.

I was once flying in a helicopter over Bloomfield Reef in the Capricorn group, on one of those bright, crystalline days that are so characteristic of the Reef, when islands hang upon the horizon like mirages and there seems no limit to the range of vision. Bloomfield Reef is one of those reefs that is only just beginning to create its own coral cay; as the helicopter approached, I could make out two linked sandspits barely visible above the water, on the edge of a superb aquamarine lagoon. There were dark blotches in the lighter blue of the reef where jagged coral occurred in deeper water; it is considered a dangerous reef by sailors. As the helicopter swooped down towards the cay I noticed a peculiar tank-track curving across the sand in a complete loop, as though something had reached this tiny bar of sand awash in mid-ocean and then turned back again. It took me a few seconds to realize it was a turtle track, no doubt made by a turtle that had come to lay its eggs on this solitary sandspit—and had been scared away.

And then, suddenly, I saw the turtle itself. It was breasting the shallow water on the windward side of the reef, several yards out from the point where its tracks re-entered the sea, plunging over the coral in a blind panic. It was I and my companions, in the helicopter, who had frightened it. Man had penetrated even here, to this remote sanctuary, and had unwittingly begun to alter the natural patterns of life. I had no wish to initiate any change, however small. We immediately climbed away, leaving the embryonic coral cay deserted.

Garden of Paradox

PHOTOGRAPHS BY WALTER DEAS

The Great Barrier Reef is an extraordinary paradox: it has a delicate beauty, captured in the photographs on these pages, and yet it also possesses a massive strength. Both qualities were apparent to Walter Deas, who took these pictures, in a dive off the reef north-west of Heron Island. Here the coral rampart drops away like a mountainside and the diver's landscape changes dramatically as he passes from the decorative coral of the upper regions, past the more rugged deeper-lying corals and down to the floor of the sea, in this case about 70 feet below the surface.

When the initial turbulence of foam and bubbles subsided after the plunge, Deas saw "a massive wall of living corals. A series of castellated islands appeared, their caves and crevices thronging with animal and plant life."

This upper level of the reef looks as soft and delicate as a garden and the coral polyps appear like plants in full bloom. Densely clustered in every shape and colour imaginable, they resemble green daisies, yellow and pink dahlias or finely-moulded mushrooms. Alongside them, the rich maroon and yellow tentacles of the tubeworms sway like fronds in the current.

Further down, the reef falls away, the glimmer of sunlight fades and the transparent blue water turns an eerie, opaque green. Here, some 50 feet down, the coral becomes at once more sparse and more spectacular: huge boulders and clumps, wrinkled as if incised with Aboriginal motifs. Even those more delicate-looking corals that survive here resemble vegetables rather than flowers—stalks of submarine celery, knobs of brussels sprouts.

Deeper still, the coral clusters peter out. The reef becomes a loose scree slope of coral debris, behind which is the solid rock, forged by the force of primeval waves and chemical changes into a massive limestone edifice. This desolate scene is so far removed from the colourful and delicate coral garden above, that it is hard to conceive that they were both built, as Charles Darwin, the great 19th Century naturalist remarked, by "the soft and gelatinous body of the polypus." Yet, "through the agency of vital laws," continued Darwin, this delicate coral animal "conquers the great mechanical power of the waves of an ocean which neither the art of man nor the inanimate works of nature could successfully resist."

POLYPS FLOWERING ON GONIOPORA CORAL

SPIRALLING TENTACLES OF A LARGE TUBEWORM

CORAL-DWELLING TUBEWORMS FEEDING ON BACTERIA

UNDERWATER MEADOW OF TURTLE GRASS

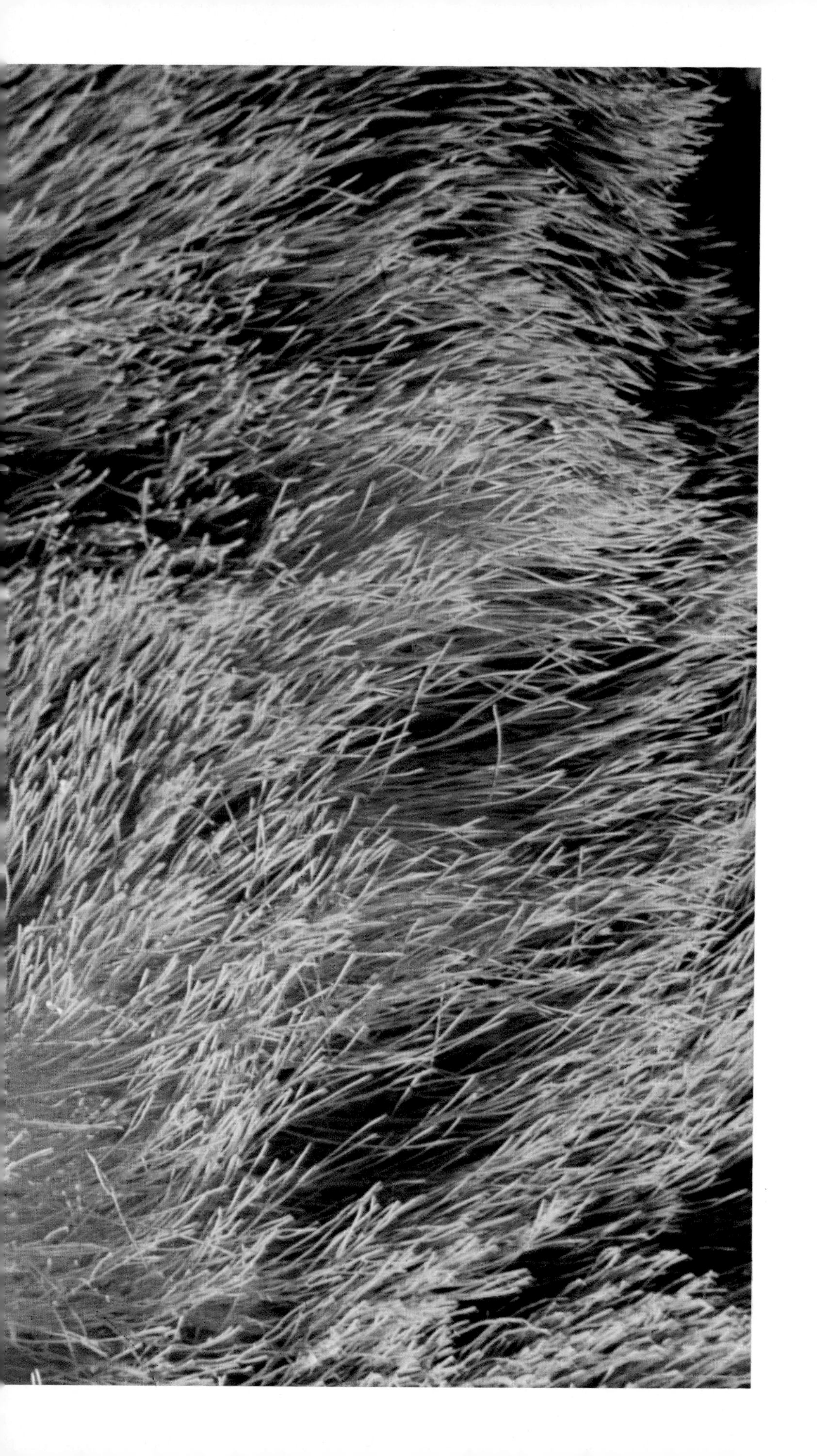

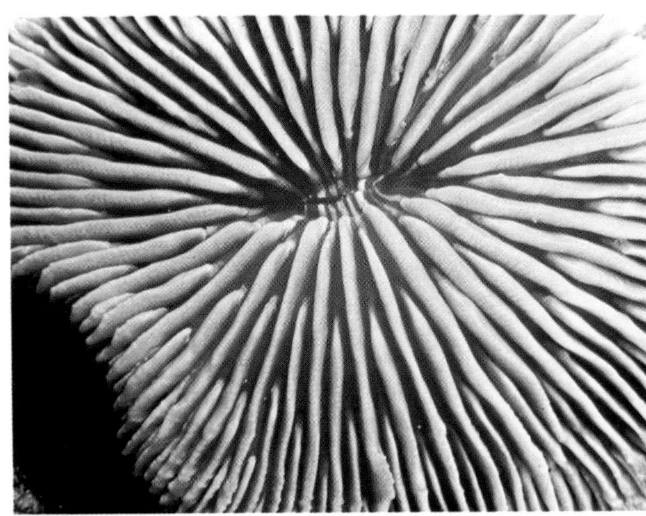

SKELETON OF FUNGIA CORAL

EXTENDED POLYPS OF TUBASTREA CORAL

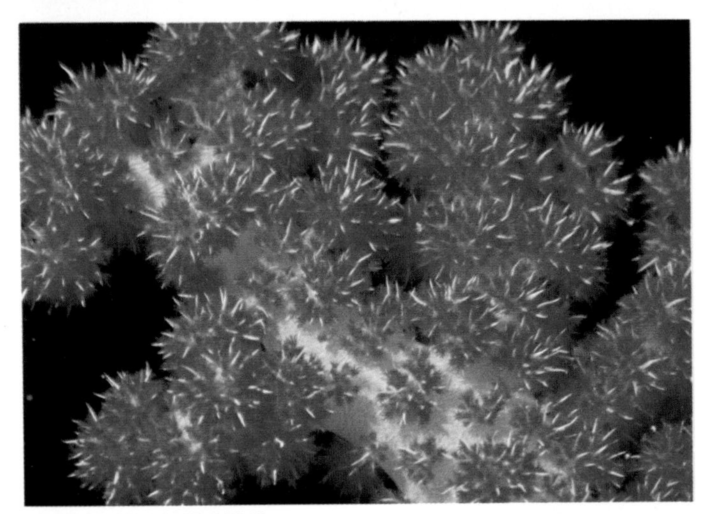

BRISTLES OF A SOFT CORAL

FAVIA CORAL WITH POLYPS WITHDRAWN

RETRACTED POLYPS OF TUBASTREA CORAL

LIME FROSTING ON FRONDS OF PADINA SEAWEED

EXTENDED POLYPS OF STYLOPHORA MORDAX CORAL

Bibliography

Allen, Gerald R., *Anemone Fishes.* T.F.H. Publications, 1972.

Baglin, Douglass and Mullins, Barbara, *Islands of Australia.* Ure Smith, 1970.

Banfield, E. J., *Confessions of a Beachcomber.* Unwin, 1908. *My Tropic Isle.* Unwin, 1911. *Tropic Days.* Unwin, 1918. *Last Leaves from Dunk Island.* Angus and Robertson, 1923.

Beaglehole, J. C. ed., *The Journals of Captain James Cook on his Voyages of Discovery. Vol. 1. The Voyage of the* Endeavour, *1768-1771.* Hakluyt Society and Cambridge University Press, 1955.

Bennett, Isobel, *The Fringe of the Sea.* Rigby, 1967. *The Great Barrier Reef.* Landsdowne, 1971.

Brown, Theo W. with Willey, Keith, *Crown of Thorns. The Death of the Great Barrier Reef.* Angus and Robertson, 1972.

Bustard, Robert, *Sea Turtles, Their Natural History and Conservation.* Collins, 1972.

Clare, Patricia, *The Struggle for the Great Barrier Reef.* Collins, 1971.

Dakin, William J., *Australian Sea Shores.* Angus and Robertson, 1953.

Dakin, William J., and Bennett, I., *The Great Barrier Reef and some mention of other Australian coral reefs.* Angus and Robertson, 1963.

Darwin, Charles, *Narrative of the Surveying Voyages of His Majesty's Ships* Adventure *and* Beagle, *Between the Years 1826 and 1836,* Volume 3. Henry Colburn, 1839.

Deas, Walter and Lawler, Clarrie, *Beneath Australian Seas.* A. H. & A. W. Reed, 1970.

Domm, Steven, *Corals of the Great Barrier Reef,* Jacaranda Press, 1969.

Domm, Steve and Alison, *A Visitor's Guide to Heron Island and the Capricorn Group, Great Barrier Reef, Australia.* Canberra Publishing and Printing Co.

Friese, U. Erich, *Sea Anemones.* T.F.H. Publications, 1972.

Gillett, Keith, *The Australian Great Barrier Reef.* A. H. & A. W. Reed, 1971.

Gillett, Keith and McNeill, Frank, *The Great Barrier Reef and Adjacent Isles.* The Coral Press Pty Ltd., 1967.

Grant, E. M., *Guide to Fishes.* Queensland Government, 1972.

Haas, W. De and Knorr, F., *The Young Specialist Looks at Marine Life.* Burke, 1966.

Holthouse, H., *Barrier Reef in Colour.* Rigby, 1971.

Idriess, Ion L., *Forty Fathoms Deep.* Angus and Robertson, 1952.

Jukes, J. B., *Narrative Surveying Voyage of H.M.S.* Fly, Volume 1. T. & W. Boone, 1947.

Lavery, H. J., and Grimes, R. J., *Seabirds of the Great Barrier Reef.* Queensland Agricultural Journal, February, 1971.

Lock, A. C. C., *Destination Barrier Reef.* Georgian House, 1955.

Marshall, T., *Fishes of the Great Barrier Reef and Coastal Waters of Queensland.* Angus and Robertson, 1934.

Maxwell, W. G. H., *Atlas of the Great Barrier Reef.* Elsevier Publishing Company, 1968.

Napier, S. Elliott, *On the Barrier Reef.* Angus and Robertson, 1934.

Power, Allan, *The Great Barrier Reef.* Hamlyn, 1969.

Ratcliffe, Francis, *Flying Fox and Drifting Sand.* Chatto and Windus, 1938.

Ray, Carleton and Ciampi, Elgin, *The Underwater Guide to Marine Life.* Nicholas Kaye Ltd., 1956.

Reid, Frank, *The Romance of the Great Barrier Reef.* Angus and Robertson, 1954.

Rippingale, O. H. and McMichael, D. F., *Queensland and Great Barrier Reef Shells.* Jacaranda Press, 1961.

Roughly, T. C., *Wonders of the Great Barrier Reef.* Angus and Robertson, 1937.

Saville-Kent, W., *The Great Barrier Reef of Australia.* W. H. Allen and Co., 1893.

Whitley, Gilbert, *Marine Fishes, Vol. 1.* Jacaranda Press, 1966.

Worrell, E., *The Great Barrier Reef.* Angus and Robertson, 1966.

Yasuda, Fujio and Hiyama, Yoshio, *Pacific Marine Fishes.* T.F.H. Publications, 1972.

Yonge, C. M., *A Year on the Great Barrier Reef.* Putnam, 1930.

Acknowledgements

The author and editors of this book wish to thank the following: Dr. Colin Braithwaite, University of Dundee; Theo Brown, Magnetic Island, Queensland; Carla Catterall, Department of Zoology, University of Queensland; Ailsa Clark, British Museum of Natural History, London; Ben Cropp, Gold Coast, Queensland; Walter Deas, Sydney; Dr. Steven Domm, Marine Research Station, Lizard Island, Queensland; Senator G. Georges, Commonwealth Parliament, Canberra; Keith Gillett, Sydney; Reg McMahon, Research Station, Heron Island, Queensland; Pamela Poulson, Heron Island, Queensland; Reference Library staff, Australia House, London; Dr. Frank Talbot, Director, Australian Museum, Sydney; Dr. John Taylor, British Museum of Natural History, London; Alwyne Wheeler, British Museum of Natural History, London; Judith Wright, Save the Barrier Reef Committee, Brisbane; Sir Maurice Yonge, Edinburgh.

Picture Credits

Sources for pictures in this book are separated from left to right by commas, from top to bottom by dashes.

Cover–Walter Deas. Front end papers 2, 3–The Photographic Library of Australia, Sydney. Front end paper 4, page 1–Isobel Bennett from Natural Science Photos, London. 2, 3, 4, 5–Keith Gillett. 6, 7–V. Vlasoff. 8, 9–The Photographic Library of Australia. 10, 11–Walter Deas. 12, 13–Robin Smith. 18, 19–Map by Hunting Surveys Ltd., London. 23, 27, 31–Keith Gillett. 32–Glen Millott. 33–Walter Deas. 34–Neville Coleman-Walter Deas. 35–Walter Deas. 36, 37–Neville Coleman. 38–Walter Deas. 39–Walter Deas-Glen Millott, Valerie Taylor from Ardea Photographics, London. 40, 41–Eric Edward. 45–Eva Cropp. 50–Glen Millott. 55 to 61–Keith Gillett. 65–Ben Cropp. 69–Neville Coleman. 73–Ben Cropp. 76, 77–Walter Deas. 83–Ben Cropp. 84–Keith Gillett. 85–Walter Deas. 86, 87, 88, 89–Keith Gillett. 92–Douglass Baglin Photography Pty. Ltd. 95–Douglass Baglin-Walter Deas. 101 to 109 Walter Deas. 113–Anthony Healy. 118–Keith Gillett, Neville Coleman from Photographic Library of Australia–Keith Gillett, Neville Coleman. 119–Keith Gillett. 123–Keith Gillett. 124–Neville Coleman. 129–Keith Gillett. 130, 131, 132–Valerie Taylor from Ardea Photographics, London. 133–Neville Coleman. 134–Keith Gillett. 135–Neville Coleman. 136–Valerie Taylor from Ardea Photographics, London. 137–Keith Gillett. 142, 143–Anthony Healy. 151–Keith Gillett. 152–Eric Hosking-Keith Gillett, Fritz Goro. 153, 154, 155–Vincent Serventy. 159–Ben Cropp, Eva Cropp. 163–Eva Cropp. 169 to 179–Walter Deas.

Index

Figures in italics refer to illustrations

Colour reproduction by
Printing Developments International Ltd.,
Leeds, England—A Time Inc. subsidiary.
Filmsetting by C. E. Dawkins (Typesetters) Ltd., London, SE1 1UN.
Smeets Lithographers, Weert. Printed in Holland.
Bound by Proost en Brandt N.V., Amsterdam.